TEST YOUR GENERAL
SCIENCE
KNOWLEDGE

$E = MC^2$

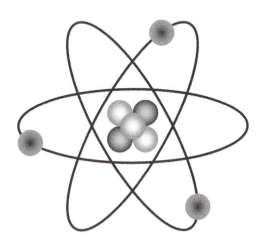

Chris McMullen, Ph.D.

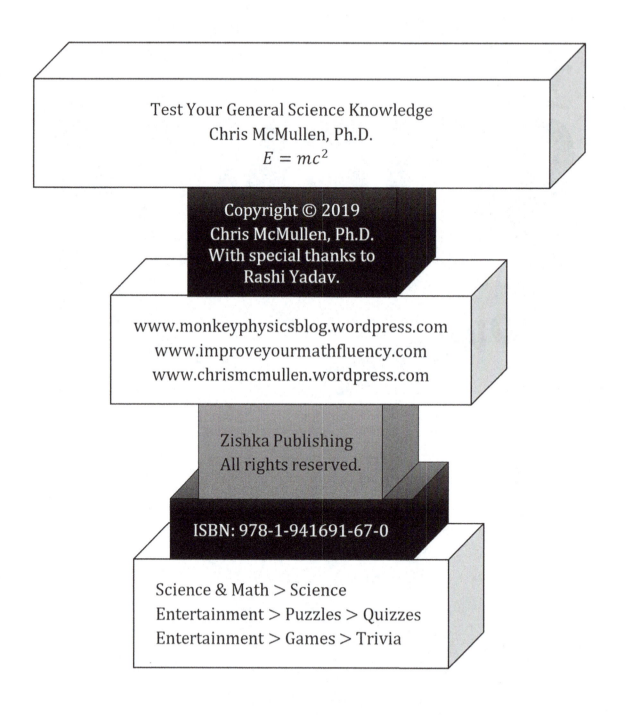

Test Your General Science Knowledge
Chris McMullen, Ph.D.
$$E = mc^2$$

Copyright © 2019
Chris McMullen, Ph.D.
With special thanks to
Rashi Yadav.

www.monkeyphysicsblog.wordpress.com
www.improveyourmathfluency.com
www.chrismcmullen.wordpress.com

ISBN: 978-1-941691-67-0

Science & Math > Science
Entertainment > Puzzles > Quizzes
Entertainment > Games > Trivia

CONTENTS

Introduction   iv

1 What's That Term? (Part 1)   5

2 What's That Term? (Part 2)   29

3 Who's That Scientist?   57

4 Give an Example   65

5 What's That Law or Principle?   75

6 What's That Number?   87

7 What Are Those Units?   95

8 What's That Formula?   99

9 What's That Concept?   113

10 What's That Abbreviation?   123

Answer Key   133

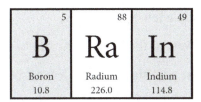

INTRODUCTION

What is the scope of your basic knowledge of general science? The chapters of this book will test your knowledge of essential topics in a variety of ways.

- Chapters 1-2 test your familiarity with common terms.
- Chapter 3 tests your familiarity with scientists.
- Chapter 4 challenges you to think of examples.
- Chapter 8 tests your familiarity with formulas.
- Chapter 9 is perhaps the most important chapter. Can you explain basic concepts?

How should you interpret the score? That's a good question. Perhaps these ideas will help:

- The usual 90/80/70 percentages shouldn't apply (unless you studied for the test).
- If you happen to be in a STEM discipline, you should have higher expectations than if you aren't a scientist, engineer, or mathematician.
- If you are in a STEM discipline, you should expect to do very well in your subject, but should have more modest expectations in other subjects.
- Each chapter starts out easy and increases in challenge along the way. You should be able to answer some of the beginning questions. If not, you've identified an area where you have good potential to improve your knowledge of science.

Can you learn science by reading this book? Here are a few suggestions:

- When you finish a chapter, check your answers at the back of the book.
- Spend time thinking about any mistakes that you made. Try to learn from them.
- If you identify a topic of interest or an area that you would like to improve, find a suitable resource to read so that you can learn more about that topic.

1 What's That Term? (Part 1)

1. What are the building blocks of matter?

2. What are the building blocks of life?

3. What are the three most common phases of matter? (Bonus if you can name another.)

4. What are the two basic types of subjects in science?

5. Which branch of science studies the earth, its composition, rocks, etc.?

6. Which branch of science studies atmospheric phenomena such as weather?

7. Which branch of science studies fossils, such as those from dinosaurs?

8. Which branch of physics studies the nature of light?

9. Which branch of physics studies the exchange of heat to and from other forms of energy?

10. Which branch of biology studies the functions and vital processes of living organisms or their organs?

11. Which branch of biology studies heredity?

12. Which branch of science studies crime scenes by applying ballistics and medicine?

13. Which steps of the scientific method can you name?

14. Which three particles are the elements composed of? Indicate the charge of each.

15. What are the five basic senses?

16. What do chemists call narrow clear glass containers about the size of a finger?

17. What do chemists call a much wider cylindrical glass container with a flat bottom?

18. What do chemists call a glass container with a wide flat bottom and narrow top?

19. What do chemists call large pincers used to pick up hot objects in the laboratory?

20. What do surgeons call small pincers used to hold tissue back or pick up small objects?

21. What do surgeons call a small sharp knife used in dissections?

22. What do surgeons call a cut made into tissue using a small sharp knife?

23. Which button on many scales lets you zero the reading for an empty container?

24. What do chemists commonly use to produce a hot blue flame in the laboratory?

25. Which handheld device can be used to detect or measure radioactivity?

26. Which term indicates how well a measurement agrees with the correct value?

27. Which term indicates how well multiple measurements agree with each other?

28. Which type of error occurs if you aren't careful how you look at a meter stick?

29. What do scientists write beside every number that they measure?

30. What is the term for which digits on a calculator should be written for an answer?

31. Which common statistical value provides a useful measure of the spread of the data?

32. What term is used to describe a substance that isn't in the solid state?

33. List the planets in increasing (average) distance from the sun.

34. List the colors of the primary rainbow from top to bottom.

35. What is a phase transition from liquid to gas called?

36. What is a phase transition from gas to liquid called?

37. What is a phase transition from solid to liquid called?

38. What is a phase transition from liquid to solid called?

39. What is a phase transition from solid to gas (skipping the liquid phase) called?

40. What is a phase transition from gas to solid (skipping the liquid phase) called?

41. Which type of organisms obtain energy by eating animals?

42. Which type of organisms obtain energy by eating plants?

43. Which type of organisms obtain energy by eating both animals and plants?

44. Which systems of the human body can you name?

45. What are the four fundamental forces in nature?

46. Which conservation laws can you name?

47. Which types of clouds can you name?

48. Which simple machines can you name?

49. What is a region of space that is completely devoid of matter?

50. What are rain, snow, and hail examples of?

51. What is the term for factors that cause an organism to react to them?

52. Which two terms are put together to form binomial nomenclature?

53. What is the binomial nomenclature for modern-day humans?

54. What are the initial substances in a chemical reaction called?

55. What is a substance that results from a chemical reaction called?

56. What is an object that travels through the air?

57. What is the path that an object follows as it travels through the air?

58. What is defined as the average kinetic energy of the molecules of a substance?

59. What is the property of sound that we hear which corresponds to frequency?

60. Which model of the solar system (incorrectly) puts earth at the center?

61. Which model of the solar system (more appropriately) puts the sun at the center?

62. What is defined as the amount of space that an object occupies?

63. What is defined as the amount of space that a container can hold?

64. What is defined in physical science as the amount of matter present in an object?

65. What is defined in physics as the resistance of an object to acceleration?

66. What is defined as the gravitational pull exerted by a massive body such as the earth?

67. What is defined as a push or a pull?

68. What are the two types of friction coefficients?

69. What is the term for the maximum speed that a falling body reaches due to air friction?

70. Which pill is given as a control when testing a drug, but has no therapeutic benefits?

71. What period of life is experienced during the transition from childhood to adulthood?

72. Which horizontal circles run east to west and vary in size on earth's surface?

73. Which vertical circles run north to south and have the same size on earth's surface?

74. What is a triangular piece of glass used to disperse light into different colors?

75. What is the term for the "rainbow" formed by dispersing light through a piece of glass?

76. Which homogeneous inorganic solids are found in rocks?

77. Which term do physicists use for the amount of a quantity without regard to direction?

78. Which term do physicist use for what you get after you join vectors together?

79. Which cells carry hemoglobin (which carries oxygen to tissues)?

80. Which cells help protect against infection?

81. What do physicists call the force exerted along a cord?

82. What is the term for a region's long-term average temperature and precipitation?

83. What do biologists call the native environment of an animal or plant?

84. What is it called when a star explodes, releasing a tremendous amount of radiation?

85. Which term (consisting of three words) includes both the brain and the spinal cord?

86. What is the name for drawing maps of the surface of a region?

87. What equals the ratio of the density of a substance to the density of water?

88. Which quantity is defined as power per unit area?

89. What is the most reactive nonmetallic element?

90. What are the two most reactive metallic elements?

91. Which element has the lowest boiling point?

92. Which is the largest currently living land mammal by weight?

93. Which is the largest currently living animal by weight?

94. Which is the largest currently living bird by weight?

95. Which is the fastest currently living, non-flying land mammal?

96. Which is the fastest currently living bird?

97. What provides a quantitative measure of the stiffness of a spring?

98. What is the term for the region surrounding the head of a comet?

99. What is the term for an equation of the form $t^2 - 4t + 3 = 0$?

100. What is the term for a membrane that allows a fluid to pass through it?

101. In which defense mechanism does a person banish anxiety-arousing memories?

102. Which type of thumb helps to grasp and use tools?

103. Which type of tail can grasp a branch by wrapping tightly around it?

104. Which term means serving to cure, heal, or preserve a person's health?

105. What is the perception of being pushed outward while traveling in a circle?

106. What is the term for acceleration (which points inward) while traveling in a circle?

107. What is the term for a number of the form [42] appearing in a published paper, which acknowledges the relevance of a particular work included on a list of numbered references at the end of the paper?

108. What is the sphere surrounding a black hole from which nothing can escape?

109. What is the term for a treeless arctic plain, covered in snow much of the year?

110. What do scientists call a mixture of two or more metals fused together?

111. Which branch of engineering relates forces or torques of systems that are at rest?

112. What is the name for a row on the periodic table?

113. What is the name for a column on the periodic table?

114. What do chemists call the electrons that an atom uses to make bonds?

115. How many noble gases can you name?

116. How many halogens can you name?

117. Which type of skeleton grows on the outside of an animal?

118. What do engineers call a functional model built for demonstration or testing?

119. What is the characteristic structure of two complementary chains of nucleotides in DNA?

120. According to Kepler, what is the shape of a planetary orbit around the sun?

121. What is the shape of the path of a projectile traveling through a uniform gravitational field in the absence of air resistance (neglecting earth's rotation)?

122. What is the lowest possible energy level called?

123. What are the higher energy levels called?

124. What is the term for a person's body rhythms as they regularly occur during a 24-hour cycle?

125. What is the outermost region of a star, which consists of low-density, high-temperature ionized gas?

126. What do biologists call a group of closely related orders?

127. What do biologists call a group of closely related genera?

128. What do biologists call a group of closely related classes?

129. Which type of chemical bond is formed when atoms share one or more electrons?

130. Which type of chemical bond is formed after a transfer of electrons between atoms?

131. What are the "classic" kingdoms in the classification of organisms on earth?

132. What is the term for the irregular motion of air which disturbs an airplane in flight?

133. What is defined as a specific characteristic of an individual organism?

134. Which explosive sound is created by a supersonic aircraft?

135. Which medical term is used to describe something that relates to the lungs?

136. What is the name of the large muscle group located on the front of the thigh?

137. Which force does a spring exert on an attached mass, pulling it toward equilibrium?

138. What are the smallest blood vessels called?

139. Which type of modulus provides a measure of elasticity in length?

140. Which type of modulus provides a measure of elasticity in shape?

141. Which type of modulus provides a measure of elasticity in volume?

142. What is the term for the plane of earth's orbit around the sun?

143. Which type of molecules do the atoms of nitrogen gas tend to form at STP?

144. Which type of rock forms when magma solidifies into crystallized rock?

145. What is the term for an animal with a spinal column?

146. What are the three basic types of galaxies?

147. What are the three methods of heat flow?

148. What do the symbols $\odot$ and $\otimes$ represent in magnetism? Which is which?

149. What is the source of a gravitational field?

150. What is the source of an electric field?

151. What is the source of a magnetic field?

152. What is the term for the diffusion of a fluid through a selectively permeable membrane?

153. Which type of twins develop from ova that are fertilized separately?

154. What is unconsolidated matter that is deposited by precipitation, wind, or glaciers, and which either comes from the weathering and erosion of rock or from the secretions of organisms?

155. What is the term for a human offspring in the uterus during its first eight weeks?

156. What is the term for a human offspring in the uterus after its first eight weeks?

157. What is the term for a fertilized egg?

158. What is the point in earth's orbit where it is closest to the sun?

159. What is the point in the moon's orbit where it is farthest from the earth?

160. Which antibiotic discovered in 1928 is produced naturally by certain molds?

161. What is defined in chemistry as moles of solute per liter of solution?

162. What is defined in chemistry as moles of solute per kilogram of solvent?

163. What is the term for the tendency of a mineral to break along a definite plane?

164. What provides a statistical measure of the degree to which two factors are related?

165. What is it called when the moon blocks sunlight from reaching part of the earth?

166. What is it called when the earth blocks sunlight from reaching part of the moon?

167. Which layers of the earth's atmosphere can you name?

168. Which layers of the earth can you name?

169. Which layers of the sun can you name?

170. What is a sequence of DNA which codes for a protein, and which determines a trait?

171. Which member of a pair of hereditary factors gets used when both factors are present?

172. Which member of a pair of hereditary factors remains latent when both are present?

173. Which threadlike structure of DNA and proteins carries genetic information?

174. Which common rapid oxidation process is accompanied by heat and light?

175. What is it called when a metal is oxidized by a substance in its environment?

176. What is it called when water or wind removes and transports soil to another location?

177. What is it called when transported material wears a rocky surface through scraping?

178. Which extinct elephant is known for its long curled tusks and large size?

179. What is it called when the visible face of the moon appears larger than the day before?

180. What is it called when the visible face of the moon appears smaller than the day before?

181. What is the term for a region of low pressure created as a sound wave propagates?

182. What is it called when a doctor removes tissue for a diagnostic examination?

183. Which branch of engineering designs, builds, and maintains public works?

184. What is a protein that speeds up the rate of a particular biological reaction?

185. What is the technical term for navel (or belly button)?

186. What is the name of our galaxy? Which type of galaxy is it?

187. What is the name of our nearest star (other than the earth's sun)?

188. Which weather phenomenon is associated with annual warm ocean water in the Pacific?

189. What are the technical terms for the Northern Lights and Southern Lights?

190. What is the term for the natural tendency of an object to maintain constant momentum?

191. Which force does the air exert on a moving object?

192. Which are the four chambers of the heart and what does each do?

193. What consists of a large number of closely spaced parallel lines and is used in optics?

194. What is the point in the sky directly above an observer on earth?

195. What is it called when reduced blood flow to the heart results in chest pain?

196. What is the low point of a wave called, which is basically the opposite of a crest?

197. Which type of material does not allow light to pass through it?

198. Which type of material diffuses light so that objects on its other side aren't seen clearly?

199. Which layer of the atmosphere contains the ozone layer?

200. What provides a measure of the tendency of an atom to attract shared electrons?

201. Which class of arthropods typically have eight legs, and includes spiders and ticks?

202. Diamond, silicon, germanium, gallium arsenide, and SiC are examples of what?

203. Which phase of the moon is less than half full, yet not new?

204. Which phase of the moon is greater than half full, yet not full?

205. Which soft tissue is found in the cavities of most bones?

206. Which group of metals includes lithium, sodium, and potassium?

207. Which metals have their d subshells partially filled?

208. Which bone disorder involves brittleness and a reduction in bone density?

209. Kangaroos, koalas, wallabies, and possums are examples of what?

210. What is the maximum displacement of an oscillation (or wave) from equilibrium?

211. What is the term for the lower jaw of a vertebrate?

212. What lies between the inner planets and outer planets of earth's solar system?

213. What is the name for a chromosome that isn't a sex chromosome?

214. What is the name for an object that orbits a moon, planet, or star?

215. What is the minimum possible temperature in Kelvin called?

216. Which force attracts the molecules of two different surfaces?

217. Which force attracts the molecules of the same substance together?

218. About which point does a lever rotate?

219. Which bone is referred to as the kneecap?

220. What is it called when neither the participants nor the research staff are aware of which participants were given a placebo?

221. Snails, slugs, oysters, and octopi are examples of what?

222. Which part of an insect lies between the abdomen and head?

223. What is the name of the belt in the sky near the apparent path of the sun as observed from earth, which is marked by a dozen constellations?

224. What is defined as a (continuous) range of frequencies in engineering?

225. Which infectious disease attacks the lungs and was previously called consumption?

226. What is the heat per unit mass absorbed or released when a substance changes phase?

227. Which retinal receptors are sensitive to dim light and detect black, white, and gray?

228. Which retinal receptors are sensitive to bright light and help to perceive color?

229. Which cell fragments shaped like disks are involved in blood clotting?

230. Which surgical procedure transplants skin without bringing its blood supply?

231. What is it called when an organism forms an attachment very early in life?

232. Which curve on a map represents points which have the same temperature?

233. Which curve on a map represents points which have the same pressure?

234. In which process does a larva change in shape and form to become an adult?

235. What is a genetic characteristic that improves an organism's prospects for survival?

236. Which instrument does a physician use to listen to a patient's heart?

237. If parallel rays of light pass through a convex lens, where will they converge?

238. What is it called when maternal and paternal chromosomes are paired together?

239. What is the term for strong magnetic effects created by substances such as iron?

240. What is defined as the rate at which work is done?

241. What are the terms for the days of the year with the most and the least daylight?

242. Which organic compound has –COOH at one end and –NH$_2$ at the other end?

243. In physics, what is a system with equal and opposite charges close together?

244. What is the name of the upper arm bone?

245. What is the name of the thigh bone?

246. Which device is used specifically to measure current?

247. What is a substance that becomes insoluble and separates from a solution?

248. Which concise statement announces the essential content of a published article?

249. Which term provides a measure of wire diameter where a smaller value is thicker?

250. In which metabolic process does bacteria, yeast, or an enzyme chemically break down a substance?

251. Lobster, crab, shrimp, and barnacles are examples of which type of arthropod?

252. What is defined as the ratio of the speed of light in vacuum to the speed of light in a medium?

253. What is defined as the ratio of the speed of an aircraft to the speed of sound in air?

254. In which type of solution can no more solute be dissolved at the given temperature?

255. In which type of image do light rays appear to diverge from the image without actually passing through the image?

256. In which common chemistry technique is a standard solution used to determine the concentration of another solution (of unknown concentration)?

257. Which flat muscle at the bottom of the chest cavity aids in breathing?

258. Which tissue in many land plants transports water from roots to leaves?

259. Which tissue in many land plants transports sugar made during photosynthesis?

260. Which type of plants have the transport mechanisms described in Questions 258-259?

261. What is the fertilizing organ of a flower called, which produces pollen?

262. What are the eight front teeth of a human mouth called, which are used to cut food?

263. Which premolar adult human tooth has two points?

264. What is the name of the giant region of circulation on Jupiter?

265. Which machine balances pressure in a fluid in cylinders of different diameter?

266. Which band of tough connective tissue holds bones in place in a joint?

267. What is the term for the alternating bright and dark spots on an interference pattern?

268. Which microscopic organisms drift in the ocean, serving as food for much sea life?

269. Which branch of medicine studies disease and the diagnosis of disease?

270. Which organs filter blood, excreting urine through the bladder?

271. Which distance-measuring instrument consists of a wheel, handle, and clicking device?

272. What is it called when different species live close together to their mutual benefit?

273. In which type of reaction does one reactant gain electrons while another loses electrons?

274. Which type of earth satellite has a period equal to 24 hours?

275. What is the specific role of an organism or species in its environment called?

276. What is the term for nearsightedness?

277. Which isotope of hydrogen contains one neutron?

278. Which star no longer on the main sequence is very bright, very large, yet very cool?

279. Which dense star has collapsed to the size of a planet, having exhausted its fuel?

280. Which two types of seismic waves result from an earthquake?

281. Which organelle in a cell is a sac that stores water, protein, sugar, etc.?

282. During pregnancy, which organ on the wall of the uterus connects to the umbilical cord?

283. Which reaction forms one compound from elements (or simpler compounds)?

284. Which (typically irreversible) reaction breaks a compound up into simpler products?

285. Which (typically reversible) reaction breaks an ionic compound up into separate ions?

286. Which electronic device displays a wave on a cathode-ray tube?

287. What is the solid, rocky part of earth's crust called, which includes the upper mantle?

288. Which term describes how a bat uses reflected sound waves to map out its surroundings?

289. Which modern physics term means the smallest possible value of a quantity like energy?

290. Which neurotransmitter is associated with pleasure and motivation?

291. Which term describes how the plane of an orbit is tilted relative to the ecliptic plane?

292. What is the term for heavy bleeding?

293. In which pendulum is a projectile fired into the pendulum bob to propel it upward?

294. In computer science, what is a step-by-step procedure for solving a problem called?

295. Torque equals force times what?

296. In which condition does irregular curvature of the cornea or lens cause blurry vision?

297. What is a wheeled stretcher called that is used to transport patients?

298. Which type of light consists of a single, well-defined wavelength?

299. Which luminous discharge is caused by the ionization of a fluid in a strong electric field?

300. What is a particle, like a proton or hyperon, which consists of three quarks?

301. What is a particle, like a pion or kaon, which consists of a quark and antiquark?

302. What is a list of corrections to a previously published article called?

303. Which triangular muscle covers the shoulder?

304. What are the smooth regions of the moon's surface called?

305. What are the ground and higher states called in the context of standing waves?

306. What is the process of bone formation called?

307. Which physics instrument with rings is used to demonstrate precessional motion?

308. Which highly luminous objects are found in the centers of some galaxies, are very distant, and feature a very large redshift?

309. Which particles have fractional spin and follow Pauli's exclusion principle?

310. Which particles have zero or integer spin and don't follow Pauli's exclusion principle?

311. Which severe psychological disorders may feature disorganized thoughts, delusions, bizarre behavior, or fragmented personality, for example?

312. Which is the largest moon in earth's solar system?

313. Which object in modern physics absorbs 100% of thermal radiation incident upon it?

314. Which quantity provides a measure of the salt content in (non-pure) water?

315. Which branch of medicine studies the use of x-rays in diagnosing and treating disease?

316. In a reaction where an enzyme is a catalyst, which substance does the enzyme act on?

317. Which theorized original supercontinent of earth broke and drifted apart?

318. What is another term for gas giant or outer planet? Which planets are these?

319. What is another term for inner planet or rocky planet? Which planets are these?

320. What are two ways to multiply vectors? (Bonus if you can name a third.)

321. Which part of the brain consists of left and right hemispheres?

322. Which part of the brain coordinates muscle movement and balance?

323. Which two kinds of angular momentum can an electron have?

324. Which white, waxy, fat-like substance is the most abundant steroid in the body?

325. Which is the tallest volcano in earth's solar system?

326. Which type of lens aberration results from colors traveling different speeds in glass?

327. Which type of lens or mirror aberration has to do with the shape of the lens or mirror?

328. What is the technical term for man-made materials?

329. In which type of luminescence is visible light emitted by excited atoms shortly after absorbing light of much shorter wavelength?

330. Which device delivers an electric shock to the heart to correct or prevent arrhythmia?

331. What is an organism's tendency to maintain internal chemical and physical stability?

332. Which is the largest asteroid in the Asteroid Belt?

333. Which term describes a person who can walk and is not confined to a bed?

334. When the Rayleigh-Jeans classical prediction for blackbody radiation disagreed with experimental results at high frequencies, which two words did scientists use to describe this?

335. What does each symbol above represent? Which is which?

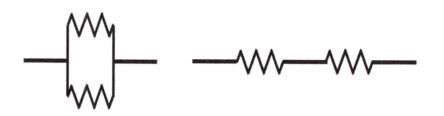

336. Which word describes each configuration of resistors above? Which is which?

337. What are the four types of nitrogen bases in DNA?

338. Which bands of the full electromagnetic spectrum can you name?

339. How many spectral series for hydrogen can you name?

340. Which geologic eons and eras can you name?

341. Which branch of zoology is devoted to birds?

342. What are the four quantum numbers for a hydrogen-like atom?

343. Can you describe any cataclysmic events in earth's history?

344. What are two types (meaning two limiting cases) of diffraction of visible light?

2 What's That Term? (Part 2)

1. What is science?

2. What does it mean to be scientific?

3. What is a hypothesis?

4. What is the distinction between astronomy and astrology?

5. What is botany?

6. What is organic chemistry?

7. What is anatomy?

8. What is ecology?

9. What is a control group in medical science or psychology?

10. What is the distinction between a dependent and an independent variable?

11. How does science define living things (that is, organisms)?

12. What is a meniscus?

13. What is the current classification of Pluto? (Bonus if you can explain why.)

14. What is an element?

15. What is a compound?

16. What is a solution? What is a solute? What is a solvent?

17. What is a homogeneous mixture? What is a heterogeneous mixture?

18. What is an autotroph? What is a heterotroph?

19. What is a decomposer?

20. What is a barometer? What is a manometer?

21. What is the distinction between psychology and psychiatry?

22. What is alchemy?

23. What is metallurgy?

24. What is the distinction between a metal and a nonmetal?

25. What are (at least) two different meanings of membrane in science?

26. What is cartilage?

27. What is bacteria? What is a virus?

28. What is a catalyst?

29. What is density?

30. What is a mole?

31. What is a tissue? What is an organ?

32. What is an artery? What is a vein?

33. How is soil defined in geology?

34. How do you determine the slope of a graph?

35. What are first-, second-, and third-degree burns?

36. What is a vector? What is a scalar?

37. What is speed? What is velocity?

38. What is acceleration?

39. What is the concentration of a solution?

40. What does it mean for a substance to be malleable?

41. What is the distinction between rotation and revolution in astronomy?

42. What is atomic number?

43. What is an era? What is an epoch? What is a period? What is an eon?

44. What is a protein?

45. What are convex and concave lenses? (Which is which?)

46. What is an esophagus?

47. What is an endothermic reaction? What is an exothermic reaction?

48. What is the distinction between a meteor, a meteorite, and a meteoroid?

49. What is the distinction between neurosis and psychosis?

50. What is a half-life?

51. What is a light-year?

52. What is an astronomical unit (AU)?

53. What does the triple point of a substance refer to?

54. What is a neuron?

55. When is there a normal force? In which direction is it exerted?

56. What is evolution? (This is asking for a definition, not your opinion.)

57. What is a comet?

58. What is a larva? What is a pupa?

59. What is an isotope?

60. What is an ion? What is ionization?

61. What is humidity? What is the dew point?

62. What is current?

63. What is an allele?

64. What is an asteroid?

65. What is a gamete?

66. What is a noble gas?

67. What is a halogen?

68. What is an orbital?

69. What is the distinction between diagnosis and prognosis?

70. What is the distinction between stress and strain?

71. What is hemoglobin?

72. What is a genome?

73. What does it mean for an object to be submerged?

74. What do benign and malignant mean in medical science?

75. What is a transistor?

76. What is leukemia?

77. What is a polar molecule?

78. What is a lesion in medical science?

79. What is torque?

80. What is a free radical?

81. What is a capacitor? (Indicate both what it does and what it consists of.)

82. What is an antigen? What is an antibody?

83. What does acute mean regarding symptoms or illness?

84. What is a biome?

85. What is ozone? What is the ozone layer?

86. What does the term aqueous refer to?

87. What is an abdomen?

88. What is an electrolyte?

89. What do the terms heterozygous and homozygous mean?

90. What is nuclear fission? What is nuclear fusion?

91. What is an organelle?

92. What is wavelength? What is period? What is frequency?

93. What is an equinox in astronomy? What are the two kinds?

94. What is a carbohydrate?

95. What is cytoplasm?

96. What are ribosomes?

97. What is the distinction between boiling and evaporation?

98. What is a nebula?

99. What is a pathogen?

100. What is energy? What are kinetic and potential energy? What is activation energy?

101. What is entropy?

102. What is enthalpy?

103. What is niacin?

104. What is a delta in geology?

105. What is a buffer in chemistry?

106. What is a confounding variable?

107. What is a black hole?

108. What is a lattice in chemistry?

109. What is pressure? What is buoyancy?

110. What is solubility?

111. What is a tendon?

112. What is a clavicle?

113. What are linear momentum and angular momentum?

114. What is cellulose?

115. What is excretion?

116. What is oncology?

117. What is refraction?

118. What is diffraction?

119. What is dispersion?

120. What is kinesthesis?

121. What is chlorophyll?

122. What is a subduction zone?

123. What is an umbra? What is a penumbra?

124. What are the dermis and epidermis (in humans)?

125. What is right ascension? What is declination?

126. What is a contusion in health science?

127. What are glacial striations?

128. What is a dielectric?

129. What is beta carotene?

130. What is a fungus?

131. What is isotropy?

132. What is glucose?

133. What is a basin in geology?

134. What is action potential?

135. What does it mean to be in remission in health science?

136. What do the terms aerobic and anaerobic mean in biology?

137. What is aerobic exercise?

138. What is the distinction between elastic, inelastic, and perfectly inelastic collisions?

139. What are longitudinal and transverse waves?

140. What is resonance?

141. What is a larynx?

142. What is the Kuiper Belt? What is the Oort Cloud?

143. What is a tumor?

144. What is a calorimeter?

145. What is agriculture?

146. What is a colloid in chemistry?

147. What is a shock wave?

148. What is pneumonia?

149. What are strata in geology?

150. What is a quark? Which flavors can you name?

151. What are mitochondria?

152. What is a photon?

153. Which specific particles are released in alpha, beta, and gamma decays?

154. What is the distinction between an acid and a base? (Don't use the pH scale to explain.)

155. What is glaucoma?

156. What is melanin?

157. What is cryogenics?

158. What is a crystalline solid?

159. What is an amorphous solid?

160. What is a chloroplast?

161. What are eukaryotes and prokaryotes?

162. What is an aperture?

163. What are hyperglycemia and hypoglycemia?

164. What is oxidation? What is reduction?

165. What is a cation? What is an anion?

166. What are a cathode and anode in electrochemistry?

167. What is basalt?

168. What are the adrenal glands? What is their function?

169. What is a positron?

170. What is an estuary?

171. What is a cornea?

172. What is a cochlea?

173. What are biotic and abiotic factors?

174. What is autism?

175. What are a stalactite and a stalagmite? Which is which?

176. What are isomers?

177. What is a transformer in electronics (not the movie)?

178. What is flux in physics? Which types of flux can you name?

179. What is viscosity?

180. What does triage refer to in health science?

181. What is riboflavin?

182. What is a bolometer?

183. What is retrograde motion?

184. What is salmonella?

185. What is simple harmonic motion?

186. What does propagate mean (in physics, not biology)?

187. What does adiabatic mean?

188. What does ablation mean in geology?

189. What is propulsion? What is thrust?

190. What is a cosmic ray?

191. What is a polymer?

192. What do the terms coniferous and deciduous mean?

193. What is a hadron?

194. What is a lepton?

195. What is isostasy?

196. What is mitosis? What are its stages?

197. What is a heat engine?

198. What are dendrites in biology?

199. What is moment of inertia?

200. What are the thalamus and hypothalamus in anatomy?

201. What is a solenoid?

202. What is pumice?

203. What is a thermal reservoir?

204. What is hepatitis?

205. What is the Gregorian calendar? What is the Julian calendar? Which is in use today?

206. What is a vestigial structure?

207. What is impulse in physics?

208. What is luminosity?

209. What is a pheromone?

210. What is an eddy current in magnetism?

211. What is a polypeptide?

212. What is Atwood's machine?

213. What do orthopedic surgeons do?

214. What is an ideal gas?

215. What is pneumatics?

216. What is entomology?

217. What is stoichiometry?

218. What do nodes and antinodes refer to on a standing wave?

219. What is the opposite of a conductor?

220. What is an inductor in a circuit?

221. What is an endoplasmic reticulum?

222. What does duality mean in modern physics?

223. What is libration in astronomy?

224. What is precession in astronomy?

225. What is dark matter?

226. What are the metacarpals?

227. What does orthogonal mean?

228. What is a neutrino?

229. What do the terms ventral, dorsal, and lateral mean in medical science?

230. What is special about the Carnot cycle? (Bonus if you can describe the diagram.)

231. What is nucleosynthesis?

232. What does polarization mean in physics? (Bonus if you can name four methods.)

233. What is arrhythmia?

234. What is a cyclotron?

235. What is an axon in biology?

236. What is a nephron?

237. What is Ebola?

238. What is the work function of a metal?

239. What is an embolism in medical science?

240. What do pair production and pair annihilation refer to in particle physics?

241. What is graphene?

242. What does it mean to normalize a wave function?

243. What are stem cells?

244. What were the hypothetical epicycle and deferent? (Bonus if you know equant.)

245. What was the hypothetical substance called phlogiston?

246. What is a Hertzsprung-Russell diagram? What is plotted on each axis?

247. What is meningitis?

248. What is a synapse?

249. What is magnetic hysteresis?

250. What is the function of the gall bladder?

251. What was the hypothetical ether in older theories of physics?

3 Who's That Scientist?

(Bonus for first names, middle initials, titles like "Sir," or suffixes like "Jr.")

1. Name two prominent Greek astronomers or philosophers to propose a detailed model of the solar system with the earth (incorrectly) at the center. (Bonus if you name more.)

2. Who observed the phases of Venus with a telescope in the early 1600's and also made notable contributions to uniformly accelerated motion?

3. Who received a Nobel Prize in 1922 for his work on a quantum model of the atom and its radiation?

4. Which Greek scientist discovered the nature of the buoyant force while determining if King Hieron's crown was made of pure gold or if it was alloyed with a less precious metal?

5. Who received the Nobel Prize in 1921 for his explanation of the photoelectric effect?

6. Which American inventor named the two types of electric charges as "positive" and "negative" in the 1700's?

7. Which Greek librarian measured the length of a shadow in Alexandria at noon on a day when there was no shadow in Syene, and used this measurement to calculate the size of the earth?

8. Who received one Nobel Prize in physics in 1903 and received a second Nobel Prize in chemistry in 1911 for research and discoveries with radioactive elements?

9. Who demonstrated that the electrostatic force between two charged particles obeys an inverse-square law?

10. Who analyzed precise astronomical measurements to determine that orbits in the solar system must be elliptical rather than circular with the sun at one focus?

11. Who published three volumes in Latin in 1687 now referred to as the *Principia*?

12. Who received a Nobel Prize in 1908 for investigating the structure of nuclei by directing rays of alpha particles toward a thin metal foil?

13. Who played a key role in developing AC electricity and designed a coil that bears his name?

14. Which **two** US astronauts landed on the moon on July 20, 1969? (Naming one is not enough, but bonus for knowing who was orbiting in the command module.)

15. Who published a heliocentric model of the solar system in 1543 in a book entitled *De Revolutionibus*?

16. Name a Greek philosopher who developed or contributed to the notion that matter is composed of indivisible particles called atoms. (Bonus if you can name two or three.)

17. Who did Voltaire introduce as the "father of the scientific method"?

18. Who invented the telephone?

19. Who is known for postulating an atomic theory in the early 1800's?

20. What are the **first** and last names of the brothers who are credited with building and successfully flying the first airplane? (Knowing just the last name is not enough.)

21. Who predicted that black holes emit radiation and postulated that the event horizon of a black hole can't decrease in size?

22. Who invented the phonograph and a practical, long-lasting light bulb?

23. Which Greek physician is considered to be the "father of medicine"?

24. Who published a work known as *On the Origin of Species* in 1859?

25. Who developed a technique to prevent bacterial contamination in milk and developed a vaccine against rabies?

26. Who coined the term "cell" and also discovered the law of elasticity?

27. Who put forth the idea of uniformitarianism when he published *Theory of the Earth* in 1795, and is considered one of the founders of modern geology?

28. Who coined the term "invertebrates" and was an early proponent of evolution?

29. Who coined the terms "dominant" and "recessive" genes?

30. Who devised in 1935 a magnitude scale for measuring seismic activity?

31. Which computer scientist invented the world wide web following research at CERN in the 1980's?

32. Who published *The Interpretation of Dreams* on psychoanalysis?

33. Which professor of biochemistry became a prolific writer of both science fiction and popular science, and is also believed to have coined the term "robotics"?

34. Who pioneered a vaccine for smallpox in the late 1700's?

35. Who proposed an absolute scale of temperature?

36. Who popularized string theory with his book, *The Fabric of the Cosmos*?

37. Who invented the stethoscope?

38. Who is credited with developing binomial nomenclature?

39. Who studied the relationship between heat and work in the 1800's, leading to the law of conservation of energy and the first law of thermodynamics?

40. Who received a Nobel Prize in 1945 for discovering penicillin? (Bonus for two or three.)

41. Who received the Davy Medal from the Royal Society for organizing the periodic table and forming the periodic law? (Bonus if you can name two.)

42. Who reported in 1928 that he had transformed deadly bacteria into harmless bacteria, a result that would lead other researchers to discover the role of DNA?

43. Name one of three researchers who published a paper in 1944 which isolated DNA, not protein as believed at the time, as the carrier of genetic information. (Bonus for more.)

44. Who received a Nobel Prize in 1962 for their work on the structure of DNA?

45. Who received a Nobel Prize in 1906 for the discovery of the electron?

46. Who discovered galaxies comparable in scale to the Milky Way in the 1920's and also devised a system for classifying galaxies that is commonly used today?

47. Who received a Nobel Prize in 1933 for the role that chromosomes play in heredity?

48. Which astronomer wrote or coauthored several popular science books and wrote the science fiction novel *Contact*, and also promoted SETI?

49. Who received a Nobel Prize in 1932 for his work on uncertainty in quantum mechanics?

50. Who proposed that equal volumes of gases held at the same temperature and pressure contain the same number of molecules?

51. Who demonstrated the wave-like nature of light in 1801 by shining light through two narrow, closely spaced slits?

52. Who did pioneering work on microscopy in the 1600's and was the first to experiment with microbes?

53. Who developed a wave equation that incorporates the probabilistic nature of quantum mechanics?

54. Which Greek astronomer proposed that the sun lies at the center of the solar system, but had his theory rejected in favor of the (incorrect) geocentric model?

55. Which scientist has an SI unit and a programming language named after him?

56. Who discovered the principles of electrolysis and electromagnetic induction?

57. Who independently described the idea of natural selection alongside Charles Darwin?

58. Who received a Nobel Prize in 1929 for discovering that electrons exhibit wave-like properties?

59. Who is known for modifying the ideal gas law to describe more realistic gases?

60. Who estimated the speed of light in 1676 using observations of Jupiter's moon, Io?

61. Who proposed in 1925 that no two electrons can ever be in the same quantum state?

62. Who conducted an oil-drop experiment to determine that electric charge is quantized and to determine the charge of an electron?

63. Who received a Nobel Prize in 1918 for his discovery that the energy of blackbody radiation is quantized?

64. Who received a Nobel Prize in 1960 for radioactive carbon dating?

65. Who received a Nobel Prize in 1986 for their work on cholesterol? (Bonus for two.)

66. Which Greek astronomer discovered the precession of the equinoxes?

67. Who is well-known for a set of four equations describing electromagnetic fields?

68. Name one of the first geologists to write about seafloor spreading. (Bonus for more.)

69. Who is credited for both producing pure hydrogen and also recognizing it as an element, and also measured the gravitational constant?

70. Who received a Nobel Prize in 1935 for discovering the neutron?

71. Who coined the term "virus"?

72. Who is credited with founding the first formal psychology laboratory, and is considered by many to be the "father of psychology"?

73. Name one of the first geologists to write about the Pangaea or continental drift.

74. Who received a Nobel Prize in 1902 for the splitting of spectral lines in a magnetic field? (Bonus if you can name both.)

75. Who wrote *Silent Spring*, which helped advance environmental science, and campaigned to ban the use of DDT?

76. Who received a Nobel Prize in 1920 for his work on heat in chemical reactions and for introducing the third law of thermodynamics?

77. Which physician discovered an area of the brain involved in speaking language?

78. Who first trained a chimpanzee in American Sign Language?

79. Who is credited for leading a research group in the 1990's that cloned a sheep?

80. Who is considered by some to be the father of modern chemistry, contributed to the chemical revolution, was a pioneer of stoichiometry, and discovered the role that oxygen plays in combustion?

81. Which scientists conducted an experiment which is now famous for failing to detect small changes in the speed of light?

82. Who discovered covalent bonding and introduced dot structures that are now named after him?

83. Which psychologist created the inkblot test that was widely used in the 1960's?

84. Name one of the recipients of the 1990 Nobel Prize for their work on organ and cell transplants. (Bonus if you can name both.)

85. Who is considered one of the founders of modern geology and stratigraphy for his work in the 1600's, which included the law of superposition?

86. Who received a Nobel Prize in 1981 for his research on split-brain patients?

87. Who received a Nobel Prize in 1979 for developing the standard electroweak theory? (Bonus if you can name two or three.)

88. Who described the rapid eye movement (REM) that occurs during sleep in 1953?

89. Who received two Nobel Prizes in chemistry?

90. Who received two Nobel Prizes in physics?

4 Give an Example

1. List at least eight different types of energy.

2. List at least three types of physical changes.

3. List at least three types of chemical changes.

4. List at least three animals that are amphibians.

5. List at least eight different types of forces.

6. List at least five different species (not classes) of minerals that aren't pure elements.

7. List at least four different types of nonrenewable resources.

8. List at least five different types of renewable resources.

9. List at least four sources of error that are sometimes good to identify in a lab report.

10. List at least five sources of error that are generally not good to identify in a lab report.

11. Give at least four rules regarding proper chemistry lab attire.

12. List at least three names of galaxies.

13. List at least eight moons in the earth's solar system.

14. List at least one liquid that forms a convex meniscus in a glass container.

15. List at least three inverse-square laws.

16. List at least five important cycles taught in science courses.

17. List at least six functions performed by cell organelles.

18. List at least four elemental forms of carbon.

19. List at least ten measuring devices common in first-year chemistry or physics labs.

20. List at least five things that a single lowercase m or uppercase M may represent.

21. List at least six quantities that are vectors.

22. List at least eight quantities that are scalars.

23. List at least six words for the babies of different types of **farm** animals.

24. List at least six fields, branches, or other categories of engineering.

25. List at least five common substances that are less dense than liquid water.

26. List at least three strong acids.

27. List at least three strong bases.

28. List at least three different digestive enzymes.

29. List at least three waves that are mostly transverse.

30. List at least two waves that are mostly longitudinal.

31. List at least four alkali metals.

32. List at least three dwarf planets.

33. List at least five elements that tend to form diatomic gases.

34. List at least three animals that experience metamorphosis.

69

35. List at least five bacterial diseases.

36. List at least five viral diseases.

37. List at least eight chemical formulas that are primarily covalent (or molecular).

38. List at least eight chemical formulas that are primarily ionic.

39. List at least four different types of weathering.

40. List at least three polar liquids.

41. List at least three nonpolar liquids.

42. List at least three types of fungi.

43. List at least three types of protists.

44. List the names of at least eight organic compounds.

45. List at least five common redox reactions.

46. List at least three forms of cell transport.

47. List at least three strong electrolytes.

48. List at least four types of psychological therapy.

49. List at least two processes where sublimation occurs in nature.

50. List at least three types of sedimentary rock.

51. List at least two different forms of radiation that aren't electromagnetic.

52. List at least four types of anxiety disorders.

53. List at least three types of gene mutations.

54. List at least four types of shapes of molecules that aren't similar to cubes.

55. List at least three types of geological features associated with plate boundaries.

56. List at least two examples of solids classified as molecular crystals.

57. List at least two examples of solids classified as covalent crystals.

58. List at least two examples of solids classified as ionic crystals.

59. List at least three rain forests found on earth.

60. List at least four observatories.

61. List at least four thermodynamic processes where one variable is held constant.

62. List at least two detritivores.

63. List at least two applications of the Doppler effect.

64. List at least three applications of Faraday's law.

65. List at least three applications of spectroscopy.

66. List at least three applications of electrochemical cells.

67. List at least three applications of nuclear radiation.

68. List at least three applications of genetic engineering.

69. List at least three applications that use silicates.

5 What's That Law or Principle?

1. Describe Boyle's law in words (not with an equation).

2. Describe Charles's law in words (not with an equation).

3. Show how the ideal gas law combines Boyle's and Charles's laws. You may use math.

4. What is capillary action?

5. What is the periodic law?

6. What is the law of reflection?

7. What does it mean for energy to be conserved?

8. What form does conservation of energy take for chemical reactions?

9. What are Newton's three laws of motion? (Bonus if you know which is which.)

10. What are Kepler's laws of planetary motion?

11. What are the three laws of thermodynamics? (Bonus if you know the zeroth law, too.)

12. What is the law of definite proportions?

13. What is Occam's razor?

14. What are Mendel's laws (or principles)?

15. What is Pascal's law?

16. What is the pressure-flow hypothesis?

17. What is Avogadro's law?

18. What is Dalton's law of partial pressures?

19. Describe Newton's law of gravity in words (not with an equation).

20. Describe Coulomb's law in words (not with an equation).

21. What is the right-hand rule of magnetism? (Bonus if you know two.)

22. Describe Ohm's law in words (not with an equation).

23. What are Kirchhoff's rules? Briefly describe each.

24. Describe Hooke's law in words (not with an equation).

25. Describe Snell's law in words (not with an equation).

26. What is the competitive exclusion principle?

27. What is the Pauli exclusion principle?

28. What is the octet rule?

29. Describe the Doppler effect in words (not with an equation).

30. What is genetic drift?

31. What is plate tectonics?

32. What is continental drift?

33. Describe Heisenberg's uncertainty principle in words (not with an equation).

34. Describe Archimedes' principle in words (not with an equation).

35. What is Olbers's paradox?

36. What is conservation of momentum? For which kinds of problems is it really useful?

37. What is conservation of angular momentum?

38. Describe the parallel-axis theorem in words (not with an equation).

39. What is the theory of acquired characteristics?

40. What is gravitational redshift?

41. Describe the de Broglie relation in words (not with an equation).

42. What is the principle of superposition in geology?

43. What is the cosmological principle?

44. Describe Gauss's law of electrostatics in words (not with an equation).

45. Describe Ampère's law in words (not with an equation).

46. What is Fermat's principle?

47. Describe Faraday's law in words (not with an equation).

48. What is Lenz's law?

49. What is the endosymbiotic theory?

50. What is Galilean relativity?

51. What is Einstein's special theory of relativity?

52. What is Einstein's general theory of relativity?

53. Describe Graham's law of effusion in words (not with an equation).

54. What is Markovnikov's rule?

55. What are the Stark effect and the Zeeman effect?

56. What is Brewster's law?

57. Describe Malus's law in words (not with an equation).

58. Describe Torricelli's law in words (not with an equation).

59. Describe Bernoulli's principle in words (not with an equation).

60. What is the principle of faunal succession?

61. What is the photoelectric effect?

62. What is the Compton effect?

63. Describe Henry's in words (not with an equation).

64. What is Hess's law?

65. What is Hubble's law?

66. What is Hund's rule?

67. What is the Chandrasekhar limit?

68. What is the Roche limit?

69. What is Bragg's law? (We'll accept an equation for this answer.)

70. What is the law of DuLong and Petit?

71. What is Le Châtelier's principle?

72. What is Huygens' principle?

73. Describe Wien's law in words (not with an equation).

74. Describe Stefan's law in words (not with an equation).

75. What is the Meissner effect?

76. What is Curie's law?

77. What is Raoult's law?

78. What is the Weber-Fechner law?

79. Describe the Hardy-Weinberg principle in words (not with an equation).

80. Describe what Price's theorem does (in the context of biology).

81. Describe the Hall effect in words (not with an equation).

82. What is the law of constancy of interfacial angles?

83. What is the principle of least action?

6 What's That Number?

1. How many **pairs** of chromosomes are contained in one typical human cell?

2. What are the values (with units) that are associated with STP?

3. What is the pH value for pure water? Which pH values can an acid or base have?

4. How much does a one-kilogram mass weigh in pounds near earth's surface?

5. Approximately, how many days does it take for the moon to orbit the earth?

6. What is the atomic number of carbon?

7. How many valence electrons does a neutral carbon atom have?

8. What is the atomic mass of the isotope of carbon that has six neutrons?

9. Roughly, how far away is the nearest star (other than the earth's sun)?

10. Approximately, how many different amino acids appear in the human genetic code?

11. Roughly, by what factor is the moon's surface gravity weaker than earth's surface gravity?

12. How many elements on the periodic table are liquids at room temperature and pressure?

13. Roughly, estimate the number of elements on the periodic table.

14. At which temperature in degrees Celsius does water freeze?

15. At which temperature in degrees Celsius does water boil?

16. At which temperature in degrees Fahrenheit does water freeze?

17. At which temperature in degrees Fahrenheit does water boil?

18. Approximately, what is the value of π?

19. Approximately, what is Avogadro's number?

20. Approximately, what is the speed of light in vacuum in SI units?

21. Approximately, what is Planck's constant in SI units?

22. Approximately, what is gravitational acceleration near earth's surface?

23. Approximately, what is the gravitational constant (in Newton's law of gravity)?

24. Approximately, what is the charge of an electron in SI units?

25. Approximately, what is the mass of an electron in SI units?

26. Approximately, what is the value of the constant phi?

27. Approximately, what is the density of water in SI units at standard temperature?

28. How many cells does one amoeba contain?

29. Approximately, what percent of earth's surface is covered with water?

30. Approximately, what percent of water is contained in the average adult human?

31. Approximately, what percent of earth's atmosphere contains oxygen?

32. Approximately, what percent of earth's atmosphere contains nitrogen?

33. Approximately, how many teeth does the typical human adult have?

34. Roughly, estimate the number of bones in a typical adult human body.

35. How many **pairs** of ribs does the typical human adult have?

36. Roughly, what is the size of a typical atom in SI units?

37. Roughly, what is the size of a typical atomic nucleus in SI units?

38. Approximately, what is the surface temperature of the earth's sun in Kelvin?

39. Roughly, what is the age of the universe according to science?

40. Roughly, what is the age of the earth's sun according to science?

41. How many periods are shown on a standard periodic table?

42. Which value in Celsius is considered to be room temperature?

43. What is the value of standard atmospheric pressure in Pascals?

44. How many grams are there in one kilogram?

45. How many centimeters and how many millimeters are there in one meter?

46. How many millimeters are there in one centimeter?

47. How many cubic centimeters are there in one liter?

48. How many square feet are there in one square yard?

49. How many centimeters are there in one inch?

50. How many bits are there in one byte?

51. How many yards are there in one furlong?

52. How many US liquid pints are there in one gallon?

53. How many times louder is a 90-dB sound compared to a 50-dB sound?

54. How many significant figures are there in 0.00032100?

55. How many moons orbit Mars?

56. How many electrons can the d subshell hold?

57. How many electrons can the f subshell hold?

58. How many years does a sunspot cycle last, on average?

59. Approximately, what are the dates of the winter and summer solstices?

60. Approximately, what are the dates of the vernal and autumnal equinoxes?

61. In which century did Benjamin Franklin live?

62. In which century was Leonardo da Vinci born?

63. In which year did man first walk on the moon?

64. In which century was Galileo Galilei born?

65. In which century did Archimedes live?

66. In which century was Isaac Newton born?

67. In which year were the first Nobel Prizes awarded?

68. When was the American educational institution known as Harvard founded?

69. Approximately, what is the speed of sound in air in SI units?

70. Approximately, what is the speed of an airplane in SI units if its speed is Mach 2?

71. Approximately, what values (in Kelvin and Pascal) form the triple point of water?

72. What is the spin of an electron?

73. What is the spin of a photon?

74. Roughly, what is the heart rate of the average adult human while resting?

75. How many vital organs does the human body have?

76. How many weeks is considered full-term for human pregnancy?

77. What are the lengths of the small and large intestines of a typical human adult in meters?

78. What is the average reaction time for a typical adult human?

79. What is the near point of a typical, normal adult human eye?

80. What is the normal body temperature of a typical adult human?

81. How much money is awarded with each Nobel Prize?

82. What is the half-life of carbon-14?

83. What is the ionization energy for the ground state of hydrogen in electron Volts?

84. What angle do the H–O–H atoms make in one H_2O molecule?

85. In the model of electron shells, which number comes after 2, 8, and 18?

86. What are the horizontal and vertical components of a projectile's acceleration?

87. What is the index of refraction for water?

88. What is the stellar classification of the earth's sun (letter and number)?

89. Roughly, what is the mass of the earth in SI units?

90. Roughly, what is the average radius of the earth in SI units?

91. Roughly, what is the average earth-moon distance in SI units?

92. Approximately, how many times wider is the sun than the earth? Therefore, roughly how many earths could fit inside a volume equal to the volume of the sun?

93. Roughly, how much more dense is the earth (on average) than water? (Bonus if you know which planet is less dense than water.)

94. How many hydrogen atoms are present in a single glucose molecule?

95. How many oxygen atoms are present in a single $Al_2(SO_4)_3$ molecule?

96. Balance the reaction $C_6H_{14} + O_2 \rightarrow CO_2 + H_2O$.

97. Which finite temperature has the same numerical value in either Celsius or Fahrenheit?

98. How many Joules of heat raise the temperature of 1 g of water from 14.5°C to 15.5°C?

99. Roughly, when did the dinosaur extinction occur according to science?

100. How many dimensions of spacetime does superstring theory predict?

101. Roughly, what is the wavelength of red light?

102. Roughly, what is the wavelength of violet light?

103. How many chambers are found in the stomach of a ruminant (such as a giraffe)?

104. About how many genes on X and Y chromosomes carry instructions to make proteins?

105. Roughly, how many DNA base pairs does the human genome consist of?

106. How many wings does a typical bee have?

107. How many years can it take for the arctic woolly bear moth to fully develop?

108. What fraction of nRT does the internal energy of a monatomic ideal gas equal?

109. What fraction of nRT does the internal energy of a diatomic ideal gas equal?

110. How long does one sidereal "day" last on Mercury?

111. How long does one sidereal "year" last on Neptune?

112. How many generations of leptons and quarks are there?

113. How does the charge of an up quark compare to the charge of a proton?

114. How does the charge of a down quark compare to the charge of a proton?

115. Which Apollo spaceflight first resulted in astronauts walking on earth's moon?

116. Roughly, what is the height of the world's tallest living tree in SI units?

117. Roughly, how many neurons are found in a typical adult human brain?

7 What Are Those Units?

1. Give three different units for temperature. Which is the SI unit?

2. Give five different units for pressure. Which is the SI unit?

3. Give two different units for heat. Which is the SI unit?

4. Give three different units for volume. Which is the SI unit?

5. What is the SI unit for weight? What is the British unit for weight?

6. What is the SI unit for mass? What is the British unit for mass?

7. Which unit is defined such that ^{12}C has a mass exactly equal to 12 in that unit?

8. Which unit is equal to $kg \cdot \frac{m}{s^2}$? Which unit (that includes **no** prefix) is equal to $g \cdot \frac{cm}{s^2}$?

9. Give two different units for angle. Which is required in the formula for arc length?

10. What are the SI units for acceleration?

11. Give three different units for energy. Which is the SI unit?

12. What is the SI unit for power? How is it related to the SI unit for work?

13. What are the SI units for density?

14. Which unit is defined as the average distance from the earth to the sun?

15. Which unit is defined as the distance that light travels in one year?

16. Which unit is approximately 3.26 times as large as the answer to Question 15?

17. What is the SI unit for period? What is the SI unit for frequency?

18. Which physical quantity may be expressed with the units kWh?

19. Give two different units for enthalpy. Which is the SI unit?

20. What are the SI units for entropy?

21. Give the SI units for **any** (your choice) variety of heat capacity or specific heat capacity.

22. What is the SI unit for electric charge?

23. What is the SI unit for electric current?

24. What is the SI unit for capacitance?

25. What is the SI unit for resistance?

26. What is the SI unit for electric potential or for potential difference?

27. What are the SI units for electric field? (Bonus for two equivalent answers.)

28. What is the SI unit for magnetic field?

29. What are the SI units for Planck's constant?

30. What are the SI units for the gravitational constant in Newton's law of gravity?

31. What are the SI units for gravitational acceleration?

32. What are the SI units for Coulomb's constant?

33. What are the SI units for momentum?

34. What are the SI units for impulse?

35. What are the SI units for torque?

36. What are the SI units for moment of inertia?

37. What are the SI units for angular momentum?

38. What is the SI unit for the coefficient of friction?

39. What is the SI unit for friction force?

40. What is the SI unit for loudness?

41. What is the SI unit for wavelength?

42. What is the SI unit for index of refraction?

43. Which base SI unit is used for luminous intensity?

44. What are the SI units for electric flux?

45. What are the SI units for magnetic flux?

46. What is the SI unit for half-life?

47. Which quantity may be expressed with units of eV?

48. Which symbol is written after the number for the magnification of a lens?

49. What are the SI units for the universal gas constant?

50. What are the SI units for body mass index?

51. What is the SI unit for inductance?

52. What is the SI unit for the work function of a metal?

53. What are the SI units for the Stefan-Boltzmann constant?

54. What are the SI units for Boltzmann's constant?

55. What is the SI unit for radioactivity?

8 What's That Formula?

1. What is the formula that relates mass to weight?

2. What is the formula that relates mass to molar mass?

3. What is the formula for converting from Celsius to Kelvin?

4. What is the formula for converting from Celsius to Fahrenheit?

5. What is the formula that relates force to pressure?

6. What is the formula that relates density to pressure for a fluid?

7. What is the formula that relates mass to density?

8. What is the formula for molarity?

9. What is the formula for molality?

10. What is the formula for percent error?

11. What is the formula for percent difference?

12. What is the formula for the percent yield of a chemical reaction?

13. What is the formula for the percent composition of an element in a chemical formula?

14. What is the formula for the mass percentage of a component in a solution?

15. What is the formula for the mole fraction of a component in a solution?

16. What is the formula for an object that travels with constant speed?

17. What is a formula for uniform acceleration? (Bonus for two or three formulas.)

18. What is the formula associated with Newton's second law of motion?

19. What is the formula associated with Newton's law of gravity?

20. What is the formula associated with Coulomb's law?

21. What is the formula associated with Boyle's law?

22. What is the formula associated with Charles's law?

23. What is the formula associated with the ideal gas law? (Bonus for two formulas.)

24. What is the formula to find the magnitude of a vector from its components?

25. What is the formula to find the direction of a vector from its components?

26. What is the formula that relates period to frequency?

27. What is the formula that relates angular speed to speed?

28. What is the formula that relates speed to centripetal acceleration?

29. What is the formula for the force associated with Hooke's law?

30. What is the formula for the potential energy stored in a spring?

31. What is the formula for gravitational potential energy?

32. What is the formula for kinetic energy? (Bonus for rotational kinetic energy, too.)

33. What is the formula that relates force to work?

34. What is the formula for power? (Bonus for two formulas.)

35. What is the formula for momentum? (Bonus for angular momentum, too.)

36. What is the formula for impulse?

37. What is the formula that relates force to torque?

38. What is the formula for wave speed? (Bonus for two formulas.)

39. What is the formula that relates radius to diameter for a circle?

40. What is the formula that relates radius to circumference for a circle?

41. What is the formula that relates radius to area for a circle?

42. What is the formula for arc length for a circular arc?

43. What is the formula for the perimeter of a rectangle?

44. What is the formula for the area of a rectangle?

45. What is the formula for the volume of a sphere?

46. What is the formula for the volume of a right circular cylinder?

47. What is the formula associated with Ohm's law? (Bonus for the power formula, too.)

48. What is the formula for capacitance? (Bonus for the stored energy formula, too.)

49. What is the formula for capacitors in series? parallel? Which is which?

50. What is the formula for resistors in series? parallel? Which is which?

51. What is the formula for standard deviation?

52. What is the formula for half-life?

53. What is a formula for simple population growth (where resources aren't exhausted)?

54. What is the formula that relates the apparent brightness of a star to its luminosity?

55. What is the formula to convert from degrees to radians?

105

56. What is the formula associated with Wien's displacement law?

57. What is the formula associated with Stefan's law?

58. What is the formula that relates nuclear binding energy to mass difference?

59. What is the formula introduced by Planck to relate energy of radiation to frequency?

60. What is the formula introduced by de Broglie relating momentum to wavelength?

61. What is the formula associated with the first law of thermodynamics?

62. What is the formula for specific heat capacity or molar specific heat capacity?

63. What is the formula for latent heat?

64. What is the formula for enthalpy?

65. What is the formula for a reaction's enthalpy change in terms of products and reactants?

66. What is the formula for the Gibbs free energy?

67. What is the formula that relates entropy to temperature?

68. What is the formula that relates entropy to the number of microstates?

69. What is the formula for (thermal) linear expansion?

70. What is the formula for the efficiency of a heat engine?

71. What is the formula for the work done along an isobar?

72. What is the formula for spectral lines involving the Rydberg constant?

73. What is Drake's equation?

74. What is the formula that relates electric field to force?

75. What is the formula that relates electric field to the voltage between two plates?

76. What is the formula for magnetic force? (Bonus for two forms of the formula.)

77. What is the formula for time constant in an RC circuit? (Bonus for LR circuit.)

78. What is the formula for the period of an oscillating spring?

79. What is the formula for the period of a simple pendulum?

80. What is the formula for index of refraction?

81. What is the formula associated with Snell's law?

82. What is the formula for the Doppler effect? (Bonus for explaining the signs.)

83. What is the formula for the range of a projectile launched from horizontal ground?

84. What is the formula that relates molarities for dilution?

85. What is the formula for the golden ratio?

86. What is the formula for the rate of a reaction of the form a A + b B → c C + d D?

87. What is the formula associated with the rate law for a A + b B → c C + d D?

88. What is the formula associated with Archimedes' principle?

89. What is the formula that relates focal length and image distance for a lens or mirror?

90. What is the formula for the magnification of a lens? (Bonus for two formulas.)

91. What is the formula associated with Heisenberg's uncertainty principle?

92. What is the formula associated with Malus's law?

93. What is the formula for dipole moment?

94. What is the formula for the height of a meniscus?

95. What are the formulas for pH and pOH? (Bonus for three formulas.)

96. What is the formula for the speed of a P wave or S wave? (Bonus for both.)

97. What is the formula for seismic moment?

98. What are the formulas for capacitive and inductive reactance?

99. What is the formula for the phase angle for an RLC circuit with AC current?

100. What is the formula associated with the Compton effect?

101. What is the formula for the photoelectric effect involving the work function?

102. What are the formulas associated with the Hardy Weinberg law?

103. What is the formula for time dilation?

104. What is the formula for length contraction?

105. What is the formula for chi-squared?

106. What is the formula for porosity?

107. Describe or write down Schrödinger's equation.

108. Describe or write down Maxwell's equations. (Bonus for two forms of the equations.)

109. What is the Arrhenius equation?

9 What's That Concept?

1. Describe the process of photosynthesis. Include the balanced chemical reaction.

2. How do the phases of the moon form? Include a diagram.

3. What causes earth's seasons? Include a diagram.

4. Describe the water cycle.

5. The earth exerts a gravitational force on the moon. Why doesn't this cause the moon to crash into the earth?

6. What is the significance of the equation $E = mc^2$?

7. Describe the metamorphosis of a butterfly.

8. What are the different blood types? What is the Rh factor? Which types of blood transfusions are possible?

9. Describe how convection works in the process of boiling water in a pot on a stove.

10. Describe the role that certain gases play in the greenhouse effect. (This question is asking for a scientific explanation of what it is, not your opinion, belief, or conclusions about it.)

11. Describe how to use a star map (on paper, not an app on a phone).

12. Explain why the sky is blue. On a related note, why does the sun appear red at sunrise or sunset, but yellow at noon? Include a diagram.

13. How does a magnet work? What happens if you cut a magnet in half? What does the term "magnetic monopole" mean? What is known about "magnetic monopoles"?

14. How does a Punnett square work? Fill one out as an example.

15. Describe the eruption of a volcano, including its cause.

16. Describe osmosis and osmotic pressure in chemistry. Give one example from biology.

17. Given that steel is more dense than water, explain how a boat made of steel can float.

18. Describe how a rainbow forms. Where is the sun in relation to the observer? Include a diagram. (Bonus if you can show how a secondary rainbow forms.)

19. Explain why solar eclipses are rare. That is, why don't we have a solar eclipse every time there is a new moon?

20. Draw and label a prokaryote and a eukaryotic cell.

21. Discuss how valence electrons are shared by atoms in the covalent bond CH_4.

22. Discuss how electrons are transferred by atoms to form the ionic bond $MgCl_2$.

23. Describe the life of a main sequence star. What are the three possible fates of a main sequence star? What determines the star's fate?

24. Describe the rock cycle.

25. Describe the cell cycle for a typical eukaryotic cell.

26. Describe the physics of a spinning ice skater who is changing her angular speed.

27. What are specific ways that aerobic exercise helps to fight heart disease?

28. What causes tides? Include a diagram. (Bonus if you can explain spring/neat tides.)

29. Describe the close relationship between the respiratory and circulatory systems.

30. What did Galileo observe with his telescope that supports the heliocentric theory and rules out the geocentric theory of the solar system? Explain. Include a diagram.

31. Describe the Doppler effect. Include an example with a diagram.

32. Describe how carbon-14 dating works. Which reaction is central to this?

33. Explain how a basic mercury thermometer works.

34. Of all the elements, what makes carbon so important for life?

35. What is the importance of nitrogen in the soil?

36. In what sense is Newton's first law of motion a special case of Newton's second law of motion?

37. Explain how the van der Waals equation modifies the ideal gas law.

38. Describe Archimedes' principle and how it relates to floating versus sinking.

39. Which weather conditions can cause a tornado? How?

40. Describe how a heat engine works. How does the cycle of a heat engine relate to the second law of thermodynamics?

10 What's That Abbreviation?

1. What does STP stand for in chemistry?

2. What does SETI stand for in astronomy?

3. What does SI stand for in SI units?

4. What do MKS and CGS (or mks and cgs) stand for in science?

5. What do GB and MHz stand for in computing?

6. What does Roy G. Biv stand for in optics?

7. What does amu (or AMU) stand for in chemistry?

8. What does AU stand for in space science?

9. What does HR stand for at a hospital (the answer is **not** hours)?

10. What does BP stand for at a hospital (it goes along with Question 9)?

11. What do bp, fp, and mp stand for in thermal physics?

12. What do AC and DC stand for in electronics?

13. What do ppm and ppb stand for in laboratory analysis?

14. What does R&D stand for in science?

15. What does HAZMAT (or hazmat) stand for in science?

16. What does REM stand for in psychology?

17. What does pH stand for in chemistry?

18. What does Ph.D. (or PhD) stand for at a university?

19. What do B.S. and M.S. (or BS and MS) stand for at a university?

20. What does NASA stand for in astronomy?

21. What does CAD stand for in engineering?

22. What does DNA stand for in biology?

23. What do RNA, mRNA, rRNA, and tRNA stand for in biology?

24. What does dB (or db) stand for in physics?

25. What does Rx stand for in medicine?

26. What does JPL stand for in astronomy?

27. What does NSF stand for in science?

28. What does FBD stand for in physics?

29. What does SHM stand for in physics?

30. What does eV (or ev) stand for in electromagnetism?

31. What does EKG (or ECG) stand for in a hospital?

32. What do IR and UV stand for in electromagnetism?

33. What does CT stand for in a CT scan at a hospital?

34. What does GI (or gi) tract stand for in medicine?

35. What does CPU (or cpu) stand for in computing?

36. What does IP address stand for in computing?

37. What does LAN stand for in computing?

38. What does USB stand for in computing?

39. What do RAM and ROM stand for in computing?

40. What do ICU and NICU stand for at a hospital?

41. What does MRI stand for at a hospital?

42. What does TNT stand for in construction?

43. What do A, G, C, and T stand for in genetic sequences?

44. Which element does the symbol Fe stand for?

45. What is the name of the compound H_2O?

46. What is the name of the compound CH_4? (It has a special name.)

47. What is the name of the compound NH_3? (It has a special name.)

48. What is the name of the compound N_2O_3?

49. What is the name of the compound Al_2O_3?

50. What is the name of the compound $CoCl_3$?

51. What is the name of the compound $Mg(NO_3)_2$?

52. What is the name of the compound NH_4F?

53. What is the name for the compound H_2SO_4?

54. What is the name for the compound $NaOH$?

55. What does an RLC circuit consist of?

126

56. What does ANSI stand for regarding standards?

57. What does ER stand for in cell biology?

58. What does CFC stand for in chemistry?

59. What do SEM and TEM stand for in instrumentation?

60. What does VLA stand for in astronomy?

61. What does LCD stand for in electronics?

62. What do LED and OLED stand for in electronics?

63. What does RA stand for in medicine (we're **not** looking for research assistant)?

64. What does UTI stand for in medicine?

65. What does XRT stand for in medicine?

66. What does PTSD stand for in psychology?

67. What do CAT and PET scans stand for in a hospital?

68. What does URL stand for in computing?

69. What does CCD stand for in electronics (we're **not** looking for closed caption)?

70. What does NMR stand for in the laboratory?

71. What does HIV stand for in medicine?

72. What does AIDS stand for in medicine?

73. What do ESR and EPR stand for in the laboratory?

74. What does ATP stand for in biology?

75. What do EM and TEM stand for in physics?

76. What do CR and CS stand for in psychology?

77. What does emf (or EMF) stand for in electronics?

78. What does PV diagram stand for in physics?

79. What does PVC stand for in engineering?

80. What does cd stand for in SI units?

81. What does CNS stand for in anatomy?

82. What does CNG stand for in chemistry?

83. What does GIS stand for in geology?

84. What does rms stand for in the kinetic theory of gases?

85. What does sonar stand for?

86. What does radar stand for?

87. What does COPD stand for in medicine?

88. What does DID stand for in psychology?

89. What do NAD$^+$ and NADP$^+$ stand for in biology?

90. What does SUSY stand for in physics?

91. What does BIOS stand for in computing?

92. What does HTML stand for in computing?

93. What do HTTP and HTTPS stand for in computing?

94. What does OSHA stand for in industry?

95. What does MSDS stand for in industry?

96. What does USGS stand for in geology?

97. What does QED stand for in physics (the subject, **not** at the end of a proof)?

98. What does QCD stand for in physics?

99. What does BMI stand for in medicine?

100. What does EEG stand for in psychology?

101. What does LASER stand for? (Bonus if you know how MASER is different.)

102. What does VSEPR model stand for in chemistry?

103. What does ADHD stand for in psychology?

104. What does IEEE stand for in engineering?

105. What does SLAC stand for in particle physics?

106. What does LHC stand for in particle physics?

107. What does CERN stand for in particle physics?

108. What do LNG and LPG stand for in chemistry?

109. What does LPN stand for in health science?

110. What do HDL and LDL stand for in medicine?

111. What does PTH stand for in biology?

112. What does PCR stand for in chemistry?

113. What does NTS stand for in engineering design?

114. What does AGN stand for in astronomy?

115. What does H-R stand for in an H-R diagram in astronomy?

116. What does CRT stand for in electronics?

117. What does FTP stand for in computing?

118. What does IRF stand for in relativity?

119. What does btu (or BTU or Btu) stand for in heat?

120. What does WAIS stand for in psychology?

121. What does ADH stand for in biology?

122. What does BEC stand for in low-temperature physics?

123. What does GUT stand for in physics?

124. What does MIC stand for in biology?

125. What does BCS stand for in semiconductors?

126. What does DVM stand for in medicine?

127. What does DVT stand for in medicine?

128. What does PSR stand for in astronomy?

129. What does QSO stand for in astronomy?

130. What does SQ3R (or SQRRR) stand for in psychology?

131. What does AMA stand for in medicine?

132. What does ACS stand for in chemistry?

133. What does AAPT stand for in physics?

134. What does ISEF stand for in science?

135. What does ASCII stand for in computing?

136. What does IUPAC stand for in chemistry?

137. What does HDPE stand for in engineering?

138. What does CMOS stand for in electronics?

139. What does ENSO stand for in meteorology?

Answer Key

1 What's That Term? (Part 1)

1. Atoms (are considered to be the building blocks of matter)

2. Cells (are considered to be the building blocks of life)

3. Solids, liquids, and gases (are the three most common phases of matter); plasma is another phase; some people add one or more other phases, such as Bose-Einstein condensates

4. Physical science and life science (are the two basic types of subjects in science)

5. Geology (studies the earth, its composition, rocks, etc.)

6. Meteorology (studies atmospheric phenomena such as weather)

7. Paleontology (studies fossils, such as those from dinosaurs)

8. Optics (studies the nature of light)

9. Thermodynamics (studies the exchange of heat); thermal physics is the study of heat, which is more general and includes statistical mechanics and kinetic theory

10. Physiology (studies the functions and vital processes of living organisms)

11. Genetics (studies heredity)

12. Forensics (studies crime scenes by applying ballistics and medicine)

13. Observation (or measurement), hypothesis (or purpose), experiment (or test), analysis, theory, and law (are common steps of the scientific method); one might also include research, prediction, model, and conclusions, for example

14. Protons (positive), neutrons (neutral), and electrons (negative) (are the particles that make up the different types of elements)

15. Sight, sound, smell, touch, and taste (are the five basic senses); if you want to be fancy, you could list these as vision, audition, olfactory, tactility, and gustation; note that some people add additional senses, such as equilibrioception (gravity/balance)

16. Test tubes (are narrow clear glass containers about the size of a finger)

17. Beaker (is a much wider cylindrical glass container with a flat bottom)

18. Flask (is a glass container with a wide flat bottom and narrow top)

19. Tongs (are large pincers used to pick up hot objects in the laboratory)

20. Forceps (are small pincers used to hold tissue back or pick up small objects)

21. Scalpel (is a small sharp knife used in dissections)

22. Incision (is a cut made into tissue using a scalpel)

23. Tare (is a button that lets you zero the reading for an empty container)

24. Bunsen burner (is used to produce a hot blue flame in the laboratory)

25. Geiger counter (can be used to detect or measure radioactivity)

26. Accuracy (indicates how well a measurement agrees with the correct value)

27. Precision (indicates how well multiple measurements agree with each other)

28. Parallax error (occurs if you aren't careful how you look at a meter stick)

29. Units (are written beside every measured number)

30. Significant figures (are the digits to write for a calculated answer)

31. Standard deviation (provides a useful measure of the spread of the data)

32. Fluid (is a liquid or gas)

33. Mercury, Venus, Earth, Mars, Jupiter, Saturn, Uranus, Neptune (are the eight planets in order from the sun); note that it ends with S.U.N.; note that in 2006, Pluto was deemed to be a dwarf planet, a large icy body that is part of the Kuiper Belt

34. Red, orange, yellow, green, blue, indigo, violet (are the colors of the primary rainbow from top to bottom) had long been the classic answers corresponding to the mnemonic Roy G. Biv, but indigo in particular is not always included now

35. Boiling (is a phase transition from liquid to gas); evaporation is **<u>incorrect</u>**

36. Condensation (is a phase transition from gas to liquid)

37. Melting (is a phase transition from solid to liquid)

38. Freezing (is a phase transition from liquid to solid)

39. Sublimation (is a phase transition from solid to gas, skipping the liquid phase)

40. Deposition (is a phase transition from gas to solid, skipping the liquid phase)

41. Carnivores (obtain energy by eating animals)

42. Herbivores (obtain energy by eating plants)

43. Omnivores (obtain energy by eating both animals and plants)

44. Skeletal, muscular, nervous, cardiovascular (or circulatory), respiratory, digestive (and excretory), reproductive, immune (and lymphatic), endocrine, integumentary (and exocrine), renal (and urinary), hematopoietic (are systems of the human body); note that the number, names, and grouping may vary, depending on the reference; you should expect to name at least 7-8 of these

45. Strong nuclear force, weak nuclear force, electromagnetic force, and gravitational force (are the four fundamental forces found in nature)

46. Charge, energy, momentum, and angular momentum (are common fundamental conservation laws); mass is a good answer if you're thinking of chemical reactions, but mass is not conserved in general (for example, when an electron and positron annihilate, producing photons that have zero rest-mass) unless you use relativistic mass; in certain contexts, other quantities may also be conserved, such as parity

47. Cirrus, cumulus, stratus, and nimbus (are four basic types of clouds), but they are often grouped by height as low (stratocumulus, stratus), middle (altocumulus, altostratus), high (cirrus, cirrocumulus, cirrostratus), and multi-level (nimbostratus, cumulus, cumulonimbus); you should have known the main roots and prefixes

48. Lever, wedge, screw, pulley, inclined plane, wheel and axle (are simple machines)

49. Vacuum (is a region of space that is completely devoid of matter); your answer should **not** discount gravity, since there can very well be gravity in a vacuum

50. Precipitation (includes rain, snow, hail, etc.)

51. Stimuli (are factors that cause an organism to react to them)

52. Genus and species (are put together to form binomial nomenclature)

53. Homo sapiens (are the genus and species of modern-day humans)

54. Reactants (are the initial substances in a chemical reaction)

55. Product (is a substance that results from a chemical reaction)

56. Projectile (is an object that travels through the air)

57. Trajectory (is the path taken by a projectile)

58. Temperature (is the average kinetic energy of the molecules of a substance)

59. Pitch (is the property of sound that corresponds to frequency)

60. Geocentric (incorrectly puts earth at the center)

61. Heliocentric (puts the sun at the center); Kepler improved upon this slightly by placing the sun at one focus of an ellipse

62. Volume (is defined as the amount of space that an object occupies)

63. Capacity (is defined as the amount of space that a container can hold)

64. Mass (is defined in physical science as the amount of matter present in an object); however, at relativistic speeds, the definition of mass in Question 65 is better

65. Mass (is defined in physics as the resistance of an object to acceleration)

66. Weight (is defined as a gravitational force)

67. Force (is defined as a push or a pull)

68. Static and kinetic (are the two types of friction coefficients)

69. Terminal speed or terminal velocity (is the maximum speed or velocity that a falling body reaches due to air friction); velocity includes direction, speed does not

70. Placebo (is given as a control when testing a drug, but has no therapeutic benefits)

71. Adolescence (is the transition period from childhood to adulthood)

72. Circles of latitude (run east to west and vary in size on earth's surface)

73. Circles of longitude (run north to south and have the same size on earth's surface)

74. Prism (is a triangular piece of glass used to disperse light into different colors)

75. Spectrum (is the "rainbow" formed by dispersing light through a prism)

76. Minerals (are homogeneous inorganic solids found in rocks)

77. Magnitude (is the amount of a quantity without regard to direction); a vector, for example, has both a magnitude and a direction (a scalar only has a magnitude)

78. Resultant (is the combination of two or more vectors added together tip-to-tail)

79. Red blood cells (carry hemoglobin); bonus for erythrocytes

80. White blood cells (help protect against infection); bonus for leukocytes

81. Tension (is the force exerted along a cord)

82. Climate (is a region's long-term average temperature and precipitation)

83. Habitat (is the native environment of an animal or plant)

84. Supernova (is when a star explodes)

85. Central nervous system (includes both the brain and the spinal cord)

86. Topography (refers to drawing maps of the surface of a region); the similar term "topology" may merit credit, though it is used in a slightly different sense

87. Specific gravity (is the ratio of the density of a substance to the density of water)

88. Intensity (is power per unit area); in some astronomy texts, this may be referred to as flux; in blackbody radiation, it may be referred to as radiance (but luminosity would be incorrect, since that is basically power, and spectral radiance is incorrect)

89. Fluorine (is the most electronegative element, and is thus highly reactive)

90. Francium and cesium (are the most electropositive elements)

91. Helium (has the lowest boiling point)

92. African bush elephant (is the largest currently living land mammal by weight); bonus points for which type of elephant (of the extinct elephants, others were larger, but if you want to add extinct animals, there were much larger dinosaurs)

93. Blue whale (is the largest currently living animal); you definitely need the "blue"

94. Ostrich (is the largest currently living bird)

95. Cheetah (is the fastest currently living land mammal); note that there is a bat that is faster, but only when it flies

96. Peregrine falcon (is the fastest currently living animal, faster than the cheetah); bonus for which type of falcon

97. Spring constant (provides a quantitative measure of the stiffness of a spring)

98. Coma (is the region surrounding the head of a comet)

99. Quadratic (is an equation of the form $t^2 - 4t + 3 = 0$)

100. Permeable (membranes allow fluid to pass through them); if you want to get picky, there are different types, like semipermeable or selectively permeable

101. Repression (is where a person banishes anxiety-arousing memories)

102. Opposable (thumbs help to grasp and use tools)

103. Prehensile (tails can grasp branches by wrapping tightly around them)

104. Therapeutic (means serving to cure, heal, or preserve a person's health)

105. Centrifugal force (is the perception of being pushed outward while traveling in a circle)

106. Centripetal (is the type of acceleration which points inward while traveling in a circle)

107. Citation (is the term for a number of the form [42] appearing in a published paper, which acknowledges the relevance of a particular work included on a list of numbered references at the end of the paper)

108. Event horizon (surrounds a black hole, from which nothing can escape)

109. Tundra (is a treeless arctic plain, covered in snow much of the year)

110. Alloy (is a mixture of two or more metals fused together)

111. Statics (relates forces or torques of systems that are at rest)

112. Period (is a row on the periodic table)

113. Group (is a column on the periodic table)

114. Valence electrons (are involved in bonding)

115. Helium, neon, argon, krypton, xenon, and radon (are noble gases); you should feel that you could have thought of at least five

116. Fluorine, chlorine, bromine, iodine, astatine (are halogens); you should feel that you could have thought of at least four

117. Exoskeleton (is an external skeleton)

118. Prototype (is a functional model built for demonstration or testing); note that a mock-up is typically non-functional

119. Double helix (is the characteristic structure of two complementary chains of nucleotides in DNA)

120. Ellipse (is the shape of a planetary orbit around the sun, according to Kepler)

121. Parabola (is the path of a projectile, if you neglect air resistance, neglect earth's rotation, and assume that earth's gravitational field is uniform – meaning to neglect the variation of gravity with altitude)

122. Ground state (is the lowest possible energy level)

123. Excited states (are the higher energy levels)

124. Circadian (rhythm refers to a person's body rhythms as they regularly occur during a 24-hour cycle); note that "diurnal" is used in a slightly different context

125. Corona (is the outermost region of a star)

126. Class (is a group of closely related orders)

127. Family (is a group of closely related genera)

128. Phylum (is a group of closely related classes)

129. Covalent bonds (are formed when atoms share electrons)

130. Ionic bonds (are formed after a transfer of electrons between atoms)

131. Animalia, plantae, fungi, protista, eubacteria, archaebacteria (are the names of

the six kingdoms in the classification of organisms on earth, in classic textbooks in the United States); some countries used monera in place of eubacteria and archaebacteria; note that some modern views group animals differently, and may not even use the term "kingdom" (but there is still merit in knowing the history of science)

132. Turbulence (is the irregular motion of air which disturbs an airplane in flight)

133. Trait (is defined as a specific characteristic of an individual organism)

134. Sonic boom (is created by a supersonic aircraft)

135. Pulmonary (relates to the lungs)

136. Quadriceps (is the large muscle group located on the front of the thigh)

137. Restoring force (pulls a mass attached to a spring toward equilibrium)

138. Capillaries (are the smallest blood vessels)

139. Young's modulus (provides a measure of elasticity in length)

140. Shear modulus (provides a measure of elasticity in shape)

141. Bulk modulus (provides a measure of elasticity in volume)

142. Ecliptic (refers to the plane of earth's orbit around the sun)

143. Diatomic N_2 molecules (are typically formed by nitrogen gas at STP)

144. Igneous rock (forms when magma solidifies into crystallized rock)

145. Vertebrate (is an animal with a spinal column)

146. Elliptical, spiral, and irregular (are the three basic types of galaxies); note that a galaxy may also be referred to as peculiar if there is a major deviation

147. Conduction, convection, and radiation (are the three methods of heat flow)

148. ⊙ (is an arrow pointing out of the page), ⊗ (is an arrow pointing into the page)

149. Mass (is the source of a gravitational field)

150. Electric charge (is the source of an electric field)

151. Current (is the source of a magnetic field); moving charge is the same thing

152. Osmosis (is the diffusion of a fluid through a selectively permeable membrane)

153. Fraternal twins (develop from ova that are fertilized separately)

154. Sediment (is unconsolidated matter that is deposited by precipitation, wind, or glaciers, and which either comes from the weathering and erosion of rock or from the secretions of organisms)

155. Embryo (is a human offspring in the uterus during its first eight weeks)

156. Fetus (is a human offspring in the uterus after its first eight weeks)

157. Zygote (is a fertilized egg)

158. Perihelion (is the point in earth's orbit where it is closest to the sun)

159. Apogee (is the point in the moon's orbit where it is farthest from the earth)

160. Penicillin (is an antibiotic that is produced naturally by certain molds)

161. Molarity (is moles of solute per liter of solution)

162. Molality (is moles of solute per kilogram of solvent)

163. Cleavage (is the tendency of a mineral to break along a definite plane)

164. Correlation (provides a measure of the degree to which two factors are related)

165. Solar eclipse (is when the moon blocks sunlight from reaching part of the earth)

166. Lunar eclipse (is when the earth blocks sunlight from reaching part of the moon)

167. Troposphere, stratosphere, mesosphere, thermosphere (are layers of the earth's atmosphere)

168. Inner core, outer core, mantle, and crust (are layers of the earth); some texts also divide the mantle into the upper mantle and lower mantle; some texts may also count other layers, such as the asthenosphere, as separate layers

169. Core, radiative zone, convective zone, photosphere, chromosphere, and corona (are layers of the sun); there is also a narrow transition region between the chromosphere and the corona

170. Gene (is a sequence of DNA which codes for a protein, and which determines a trait)

171. Dominant (allele gets used when it is present)

172. Recessive (allele remains latent when both are present)

173. Chromosome (is the threadlike structure of DNA and proteins which carries genetic information)

174. Combustion (can come in the form of rapid oxidation accompanied by heat and light, but can also come in other forms)

175. Corrosion (occurs when a metal is oxidized by a substance in its environment)

176. Erosion (occurs when water or wind removes soil and transports the soil to a different location)

177. Abrasion (erodes a rocky surface over a long period of time as material that is being transported rubs and scrapes against the surface)

178. Mammoth (is an extinct elephant known for its long curled tusks and large size); bonus if you thought of both mammoths and mastodons

179. Waxing (occurs when the visible face of the moon appears larger)

180. Waning (occurs when the visible face of the moon appears smaller)

181. Rarefaction (is a region of low pressure created as a sound wave propagates); a sound wave creates alternate regions of compression and rarefaction

182. Biopsy (involves removing tissue for a diagnostic examination)

183. Civil engineering (designs, builds, and maintains public works)

184. Enzyme (is a protein that speeds up the rate of a particular biological reaction)

185. Umbilicus (is the technical term for navel or belly button)

186. Milky Way, which is a spiral galaxy (are the name and type of our galaxy); if you want to be more precise, it is a barred spiral galaxy

187. Proxima Centauri of the Alpha Centauri system (is the star nearest to our sun)

188. El Niño (is associated with annual warm ocean water in the Pacific)

189. Aurora Borealis and Aurora Australis (are the Northern and Southern Lights)

190. Inertia (is the natural tendency of an object to maintain constant momentum); note that momentum is mass times velocity, so for an object with constant mass, we could say that inertia is the natural tendency to maintain constant velocity

191. Air resistance, air drag, or air friction (are various terms used to describe the force that air exerts on a moving object); wind resistance is occasionally used, too

192. Left atrium, right atrium, left ventricle, right ventricle (are the four chambers of the heart); the ventricles pump blood into the arteries, while the atria receive blood from the body

193. Grating (consists of a large number of closely spaced parallel lines and is used in optics)

194. Zenith (is the point in the sky directly above an observer on earth)

195. Angina (is when reduced blood flow to the heart results in chest pain)

196. Trough (is the low point of a wave, which is basically the opposite of a crest)

197. Opaque (materials do not allow light to pass through them)

198. Translucent (materials diffuse light so that objects on the other side can't be seen clearly)

199. Stratosphere (is the layer of the atmosphere that contains the ozone layer)

200. Electronegativity (provides a measure of the tendency of an atom to attract shared electrons)

201. Arachnida (is the class of arthropods that typically have eight legs, and includes spiders and ticks); if your answer is "arachnid," that's close enough

202. Semiconductors (include diamond, silicon, germanium, gallium arsenide, etc.)

203. Crescent (is a phase of the moon less than half full, yet not new)

204. Gibbous (is a phase of the moon greater than half full, yet not full)

205. Bone marrow (is soft tissue found in the cavities of most bones)

206. Alkali metals (include Li, Na, K, Rb, Cs, and Fr)

207. Transition metals or transition elements (have their *d* subshells partially filled)

208. Osteoporosis (involves brittleness and a reduction in bone density)

209. Marsupials (include kangaroos, koalas, wallabies, and possums)

210. Amplitude (is the maximum displacement from equilibrium)

211. Mandible (is the lower jaw of a vertebrate)

212. Asteroid Belt (lies between Mars and Jupiter)

213. Autosome or autosomal chromosome (isn't a sex chromosome)

214. Satellite (is an object that orbits a moon, planet, or star)

215. Absolute zero (is the minimum possible temperature in Kelvin)

216. Adhesion (attracts the molecules of two different surfaces)

217. Cohesion (attracts the molecules of the same substance together)

218. Fulcrum (is the point about which a lever rotates); hinge will suffice

219. Patella (is referred to as the kneecap)

220. Double blind procedure (occurs when neither the participants nor the research staff is aware of which participants were given a placebo)

221. Mollusks (include snails, slugs, oysters, and octopi)

222. Thorax (lies between the abdomen and head of an insect)

223. Zodiac (is the belt in the sky near the apparent path of the sun as observed from earth, which is marked by a dozen constellations)

224. Bandwidth (is a range of frequencies, a term used in engineering)

225. Tuberculosis (is an infectious disease that attacks the lungs, which was previously called consumption)

226. Latent heat (is the heat per unit mass absorbed or released when a substance changes phase); types are heat of fusion, heat of vaporization, heat of sublimation

227. Rods (are retinal receptors sensitive to dim light)

228. Cones (are retinal receptors are sensitive to bright light)

229. Platelets (are involved in blood clotting)

230. Grafting (transplants skin without bringing its blood supply); in contrast, flap surgery brings the blood supply

231. Imprinting (occurs when an organism forms an attachment very early in life)

232. Isotherm (is a curve on a map where points have the same temperature)

233. Isobar (is a curve on a map where points have the same pressure)

234. Metamorphosis (occurs when a larva changes form to become an adult)

235. Adaptation (is a genetic characteristic that improves an organism's prospects for survival)

236. Stethoscope (is used by a physician to listen to a patient's heart)

237. Focus (is the point where such rays converge)

238. Homologous (is when maternal and paternal chromosomes are paired together)

239. Ferromagnetism (refers to strong magnetic effects created by substances such as iron)

240. Power (is the rate at which work is done)

241. Summer and winter solstice (are the days of the year with the most and least daylight)

242. Amino acid (is an organic compound with $-COOH$, which is a carboxyl group, at one end and $-NH_2$, which is an amino group, at the other end)

243. Dipole (is a system with equal and opposite charges close together)

244. Humerus (is the upper arm bone)

245. Femur (is the thigh bone)

246. Ammeter (measures current); note that a multimeter can measure more than just current

247. Precipitate (is a substance that is at first slightly soluble, then becomes insoluble and separates from a solution)

248. Abstract (is a concise statement which announces the essential content of a published article)

249. Gauge (provides a measure of wire diameter where a smaller value is thicker); for example, 16 gauge wire is thicker than 20 gauge wire

250. Fermentation (is a metabolic process in which bacteria, yeast, or an enzyme chemically breaks down a substance)

251. Crustaceans (include lobster, crab, shrimp, and barnacles)

252. Index of refraction (is the ratio of the speed of light in vacuum to the speed of light in a medium)

253. Mach number (is the ratio of the speed of an aircraft to the speed of sound in air)

254. Saturated solutions (are solutions where no more solute can be dissolved at the given temperature)

255. Virtual image (is an image where light rays appear to diverge from the image without actually passing through the image)

256. Titration (uses a standard solution to determine the concentration of another solution of unknown concentration)

257. Diaphragm (is a flat muscle at the bottom of the chest cavity which aids in breathing); the midriff also refers to this part of the body

258. Xylem (is vascular tissue in many land plants which transports water from roots to leaves)

259. Phloem (is vascular tissue in many land plants which transports sugar made during photosynthesis)

260. Vascular plants (have xylem and phloem)

261. Stamen (is the fertilizing organ of a flower, which produces pollen); note that the anther is the part of the stamen which contains the pollen

262. Incisors (are the eight front teeth of a human mouth, which are used to cut food)

263. Bicuspid (is a premolar adult human tooth with two points or cusps)

264. Great Red Spot (is the giant region of circulation on Jupiter)

265. Hydraulic press (balances pressure in a fluid in cylinders of different diameter); it is analogous to a lever, but balances pressure rather than torque

266. Ligament (is a band of tough connective tissue that holds bones in place in a joint)

267. Fringes (are alternating bright and dark spots on an interference pattern); they are also referred to as positions of constructive or destructive interference

268. Plankton (are microscopic organisms that drift in the ocean, serving as food for much sea life)

269. Pathology (studies disease and the diagnosis of disease)

270. Kidneys (are organs that filter blood, excreting urine through the bladder)

271. Trundle wheel (has a handle and clicking device, and measures distance)

272. Symbiosis or symbiotic relationship (is when different species live close together to their mutual benefit)

273. Oxidation-reduction reaction, or redox for short (is a reaction in which one reactant gain electrons, becoming reduced, while another loses electrons, becoming oxidized; note that a gain of electrons means "reduced" in the sense that it makes the charge more negative, which means that the charge is less positive)

274. Geosynchronous (refers to an earth satellite with a period equal to 24 hours)

275. Niche (is the specific role of an organism or species in its environment)

276. Myopia (means nearsightedness)

277. Deuterium (is an isotope of hydrogen containing one neutron); note that the most abundant form of hydrogen has zero neutrons (all forms have one proton)

278. Red giant (is a star no longer on the main sequence that is very bright, very

large, yet very cool); a red giant is very bright because it has high luminosity, yet it is very cool because red stars have lower surface temperatures

279. White dwarf (is a dense star that has collapsed to the size of a planet, having exhausted its fuel); it is initially very hot and bright, however it gradually cools down until it eventually becomes a black dwarf

280. P (primary) and S (secondary) waves (are types of seismic waves)

281. Vacuole (is an organelle in a cell which is a sac that stores water, protein, sugar, etc.); note that eukaryotic cells have vesicles, which are much smaller sacs

282. Placenta (is an organ on the wall of the uterus which connects to the umbilical cord during pregnancy)

283. Synthesis (forms a compound from elements or simpler compounds); it has the structure $A + B \rightarrow C$

284. Decomposition (breaks a compound up into simpler products, and is typically irreversible); it has the structure $A \rightarrow B + C$

285. Dissociation (breaks an ionic compound up into separate ions, and is typically reversible); an example is $NaCl \rightarrow Na^+ + Cl^-$ (but note that dissociation has a more general meaning than is illustrated by this question)

286. Oscilloscope (displays a wave on a cathode-ray tube)

287. Lithosphere (is the solid, rocky part of earth's crust, which includes the upper mantle); it consists of both the crust and the upper mantle (in common contexts)

288. Echolocation (describes how a bat, as well as some other animals, uses reflected sound waves to map out its surroundings)

289. Quantum (means the smallest possible value of a quantity that is quantized, such as energy or angular momentum)

290. Dopamine (is a neurotransmitter associated with pleasure and motivation)

291. Inclination (is the angle between the plane of an orbit and the ecliptic plane)

292. Hemorrhage (is heavy bleeding)

293. Ballistic pendulum (involves firing a projectile into the pendulum bob, which may be a block of wood, to propel it upward)

294. Algorithm (is a step-by-step procedure for solving a problem); note that an algorithm consists of a set of ideas expressed as written instructions, whereas a program implements these instructions in a specific language (like Python or BASIC) and is executed to solve the problem (in contrast, an algorithm might be written in plain English)

295. Lever arm (multiplies force to make torque)

296. Astigmatism (is a condition where irregular curvature of the cornea or lens causes blurry vision)

297. Gurney (is a wheeled stretcher that is used to transport patients)

298. Monochromatic (light consists of a single, well-defined wavelength); note that a single wavelength corresponds to a single color (except that wavelength is more general than color, since most of the electromagnetic spectrum is invisible to the eye)

299. Corona discharge (is caused by the ionization of a fluid in a strong electric field, often near the sharp point of a conductor at a high electric potential; in many instances of corona discharge, the fluid is the air)

300. Baryon (consists of three quarks or three antiquarks; examples include the proton, neutron, and hyperon); note that a nucleon is a particle contained in the nucleus, such as a proton or neutron, but does not correctly answer the question since a hyperon is not a nucleon

301. Meson (consists of a quark and antiquark; examples include the pion and kaon)

302. Errata (is a list of corrections to a previously published article)

303. Deltoid (is a triangular muscle that covers the shoulder)

304. Maria (are smooth regions of the moon's surface); note that mare is singular

305. One common naming scheme calls these the fundamental, first overtone, second

overtone, etc., while another common naming scheme calls these the first harmonic, second harmonic, third harmonic, etc. (the ground and higher states in the context of standing waves)

306. Ossification or osteogenesis (is the process of bone formation)

307. Gyroscope (is a physics instrument which consists of a set of rings that can spin in different directions, which is used to demonstrate precessional motion)

308. Quasars or quasi-stellar objects (are highly luminous objects found in the centers of some galaxies, are very distant, and feature a very large redshift)

309. Fermions (have fractional spin and follow Pauli's exclusion principle), which include leptons, such as the electron, as well as quarks and baryons, for example

310. Bosons (have zero or integer spin and don't follow Pauli's exclusion principle), which include the photon, gluon, and mesons, for example

311. Schizophrenia (is a group of severe psychological disorders which may feature disorganized thoughts, delusions, bizarre behavior, or fragmented personality)

312. Ganymede (is the largest moon in earth's solar system); note that Ganymede (which is Jupiter's largest moon) is larger than Titan (which is Saturn's largest moon), even though Titan is named after giant and powerful Greek gods (surely, that's why many astronomy students who didn't study quite enough guess this incorrectly); it may help to note that Ganymede, Titan, and Triton (Neptune's largest moon) are alphabetical when ordered in size from largest to smallest (but not for Uranus)

313. Black body (is an object that absorbs 100% of incident thermal radiation); thus, a black body is a perfect absorber (and is also a perfect emitter)

314. Salinity (provides a measure of the salt content in water, where in this context by "water" we don't mean pure H_2O)

315. Radiology (studies the use of x-rays and other forms of radiation in diagnosing and treating disease)

316. Substrate or enzyme substrate (is the substance that an enzyme acts on in a reaction where the enzyme serves as a catalyst)

317. Pangaea (is the theorized original supercontinent of earth, which has long since broken up and drifted apart)

318. Jovian planet (is a gas giant or outer planet), which includes Jupiter, Saturn, Uranus, and Neptune

319. Terrestrial planet (is an inner planet), which includes Mercury, Venus, Earth, and Mars

320. Scalar product and vector product, also called the dot product and cross product (are two ways to multiply vectors); in the context of matrices, a third method is the outer product (which isn't used by students nearly as often as the other methods; but it is useful in certain types of proofs in linear algebra)

scalar product, aka inner product: $(A_x \quad A_y \quad A_z)\begin{pmatrix} B_x \\ B_y \\ B_z \end{pmatrix} = A_x B_x + A_y B_y + A_z B_z$

vector product: $\begin{vmatrix} \hat{\mathbf{i}} & \hat{\mathbf{j}} & \hat{\mathbf{k}} \\ A_x & A_y & A_z \\ B_x & B_y & B_z \end{vmatrix}$

outer product: $\begin{pmatrix} A_x \\ A_y \\ A_z \end{pmatrix}(B_x \quad B_y \quad B_z) = \begin{pmatrix} A_x B_x & A_x B_y & A_x B_z \\ A_y B_x & A_y B_y & A_y B_z \\ A_z B_x & A_z B_y & A_z B_z \end{pmatrix}$

321. Cerebrum (is the part of the brain consisting of left and right hemispheres)

322. Cerebellum (coordinates muscle movement and balance)

323. Spin angular momentum and orbital angular momentum (are the two types of angular momentum that an electron can have)

324. Cholesterol (is a white, waxy, fat-like substance, and is the most abundant steroid in the body)

325. Olympus Mons on Mars (is the tallest volcano in earth's solar system); although

Olympus Mons is the tallest volcano in the solar system, it might not be the tallest mountain now that a very tall mountain has been found on the asteroid Vesta

326. Chromatic aberration (results from colors traveling different speeds in glass, since the index of refraction of glass varies slightly for different wavelengths)

327. Spherical aberration (has to do with the shape of the lens or mirror)

328. Synthetic materials (are man-made materials)

329. Fluorescence (is where excited atoms emit light, usually visible, shortly after absorbing light of much shorter wavelength, usually ultraviolet or x-ray); perhaps you should also receive credit for phosphorescence, even though in that case the luminescence occurs on a longer time scale

330. Defibrillator (is a device that delivers an electric shock to the heart to correct or prevent arrhythmia); pacemaker may also merit credit

331. Homeostasis (is the tendency of an organism to maintain internal chemical and physical stability by compensating for changes in the environment)

332. Ceres (is the largest asteroid in our solar system)

333. Ambulatory (refers to a person who can walk and is not confined to a bed)

334. Ultraviolet catastrophe (refers to the disagreement between the Rayleigh-Jeans classical prediction for blackbody radiation and experimental results for when the frequency is high)

335. Biological hazard aka biohazard (left)

ionizing radiation (right); sometimes called radioactivity warning

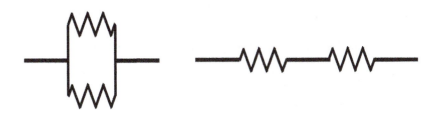

336. Parallel (left) and series (right)

337. Adenine, guanine, cytosine, and thymine (are the nitrogen bases in DNA)

338. Gamma rays, x-rays, ultraviolet, visible, infrared, microwave, radio waves (are bands in the electromagnetic spectrum)

339. Balmer, Lyman, Paschen, Brackett, Pfund, Humphreys (are series of spectral lines for hydrogen)

340. Hadean, Archean, Proterozoic, and Phanerozoic are eons (the first three are collectively known as Precambrian)

Archean eon includes the Eoarchean, Paleoarchean, Mesoarchean, Neoarchean eras

Proterozoic eon includes Paleoproterozoic, Mesoproterozoic, Neoproterozoic eras

Phanerozoic eon includes Paleozoic, Mesozoic, Cenozoic eras

Hadean eon isn't divided into eras

bonus for knowing some of the epochs (some of which may be more widely known than the eons or eras), such as Jurassic, Cretaceous, and Holocene, or for knowing some of the periods, such as Quaternary (but also note that there have been naming and division changes with the periods)

341. Ornithology (is the branch of zoology devoted to birds)

342. n = principal quantum number (for energy), ℓ = azimuthal quantum number (for the magnitude of the electron's angular momentum), m_ℓ = magnetic quantum number (for the direction of the electron's angular momentum), and m_s = spin quantum number (for the electron's spin angular momentum, which may be spin up or spin down)

343. Permian-Triassic extinction about 250 million years ago (dinosaurs appeared)

Impact in Yucatán Peninsula about 65 million years ago (dinosaurs became extinct)

Triassic-Jurassic extinction 200 million years ago

Denovian extinction event 360 million years ago

Ordovician-Silurian extinction 440 million years ago

(are five cataclysmic events in earth's history, listed in a 1982 paper by Jack Sepkoski and David M. Raup)

344. Fresnel and Fraunhofer (are two types of diffraction)

2 What's That Term? (Part 2)

1. Science is the study of nature and the physical world using a systematic approach based on observation and experiment (i.e. the scientific method).

2. Scientific essentially means that it can be tested. The main idea driven home in science textbooks for non-scientists is that a statement is scientific if you can test it.

3. A hypothesis is not a completely blind guess, but is educated in some way.

4. Astronomy applies the scientific method to study the universe. Astrology begins by assuming that the positions of heavenly bodies impact the lives of humans.

5. Botany is the study of plants.

6. Organic chemistry is the study of compounds that contain carbon.

7. Anatomy is the study of an organism's body.

8. Ecology is the study of the relationship between organisms and their environment.

9. In medical science or psychology, a control group does **not** receive the treatment.

10. The independent variable is the factor that is manipulated during an experiment. The dependent variable changes in response to this manipulation.

11. Living things (or organisms) respond to stimuli, grow and develop, consume energy, use resources, reproduce, and are based on a basic building block (a cell).

12. A meniscus refers to the curved upper surface of a liquid in a container.

13. Pluto is a dwarf planet, largely because it hasn't cleared matter from its orbit.

14. An element can't be broken down to a simpler structure using chemical means. The elements are different types of atoms.

15. A compound consists of two or more elements bound together in a definite proportion.

16. A solution is a homogeneous mixture of two or more substances. One substance (the solute) is dissolved in another (the solvent) to form the solution.

17. A homogenous mixture has a uniform distribution, unlike heterogeneous.

18. An autotroph produces its own food (like plants and certain types of bacteria). A heterotroph gets its food from other organisms (plants or animals).

19. A decomposer breaks down an organism that is dead or decomposing.

20. A barometer measures atmospheric pressure. A manometer measures the pressure of a fluid (which may or may not be the atmosphere).

21. Psychology is the study of behavior and the mind. Psychiatry is a branch of medical science that studies psychological disorders and is practiced by physicians.

22. Alchemy was an early form of chemistry attempting to turn metals into gold.

23. Metallurgy is the branch of science that studies metals, including their purification (separation from ores) and production (for example, making alloys).

24. Metals tend to have a luster, be malleable, be ductile, be opaque, and be good conductors of both electricity and heat, unlike nonmetals.

25. A membrane could be a thin, flexible material serving as a filter (for example, in osmosis), it could be the thin structure that surrounds a cell (a cell membrane), or it could be a thin layer of cells that serves as a lining in a plant or animal.

26. Cartilage is a firm, yet flexible connective tissue found (for example) in joints.

27. Bacteria are unicellular prokaryotes with cell walls that contain peptidoglycan, which can survive in many different types of environments. A virus is a structure

that is smaller than bacteria, consisting of protons and nucleic acids (and sometimes lipids), which generally needs a host (plant or animal). Antibiotics may kill bacteria, but aren't effective against a virus.

28. A catalyst is a substance that affects the rate of a reaction (usually by speeding it up) without undergoing a (permanent) chemical change.

29. Density is mass per unit volume, which provides a measure of compactness.

30. A mole is a collection of entities equal to Avogadro's number, 6.022×10^{23}.

31. Tissue consists of similar cells performing a similar function. An organ consists of tissues working together to perform functions that are closely related.

32. An artery is a large blood vessel in which blood travels away from the heart. A vein is a large blood vessel in which blood returns to the heart.

33. Soil is the surface layer of the earth that supports plant life, and which consists of minerals, organic matter, water, and air.

34. The slope of a graph equals the rise divided by the run.

35. A first-degree burn involves reddening of the skin, a second-degree burn also has blisters, and a third-degree burn destroys skin and affects deeper tissues.

36. A vector includes both a magnitude and direction. A scalar has a magnitude, but not direction. (The more technical distinction involves a coordinate transformation.)

37. Speed is a measure of how fast an object moves (the instantaneous time rate of change of position). Velocity is a combination of speed and direction.

38. Acceleration is a measure of how velocity changes (the instantaneous time rate of change of velocity), including changes in speed and changes in direction.

39. Concentration is the amount of solute present in a given amount of solvent or solution. There are different forms of concentration, such as molarity and molality.

40. Malleable means that a substance can change shape by hammering (for example) without breaking.

41. Rotation occurs when a body spins on its axis (like the earth completing one rotation on its axis every 24 hours), whereas revolution refers to a body that travels in an orbit (like the earth completing one revolution around the sun every 365 days).

42. Atomic number refers to the number of protons in the nucleus of an atom.

43. An eon is the longest unit of geologic time, followed by an era, a period, and an epoch. Bonus if you know how it is based on rock strata.

44. A protein is complex polymer consisting of long chains of amino acids, which is found in cells and which is an essential part of animals' diets.

45. A convex lens curves outward in the middle and causes parallel rays of light to converge at a focus. A concave lens is narrower in its middle region and causes parallel rays of light to diverge away from a focus.

46. An esophagus is a tube extending from the mouth to the stomach.

47. An endothermic reaction absorbs energy. An exothermic reaction releases it.

48. A chunk of rock smaller than an asteroid is called a meteoroid out in space, a meteor as it burns while passing through the atmosphere, and a meteorite after it lands on the surface of a planet or moon.

49. Neurosis is a mental disorder where a symptom causes psychological pain, and psychosis is a mental disorder where reality is distorted, such as through irrational thoughts, delusions, or hallucinations.

50. Half-life is the time it takes for one-half of a sample to decay.

51. One light-year is the distance (**not** a time) that light travels in one year.

52. One astronomical unit (AU) equals the average earth-sun distance.

53. Triple point (of a substance) refers to the combination of pressure and temperature for which the solid, liquid, and gaseous phases coexist in equilibrium.

54. A neuron is a nerve cell.

55. When an object is in contact with a surface, the surface exerts a normal force

on the object which is perpendicular to the surface.

56. Evolution is the process by which, according to modern scientists, organisms have descended from previous organisms.

57. A comet is a body (typically icy) that orbits the sun in a highly elliptical orbit, and which develops a coma and tail when passing near enough to the sun.

58. In the metamorphosis of an insect, the larva is the juvenile form and the pupa is the form it takes between the larva and adult forms.

59. Two isotopes of the same element differ in the number of neutrons.

60. An ion is an atom that has more or fewer electrons than protons, and thus has a net charge. Ionization is the process by which an ion is formed.

61. Humidity provides a measure of how much water vapor is in the air. The dew point is the temperature below which dew can form.

62. Current is the rate of flow of charge.

63. An allele is one of two (or more) forms of a gene located at the same position on a chromosome.

64. An asteroid is a rocky body that orbits a star, which is smaller than a planet, but larger than a meteoroid.

65. A gamete is a reproductive cell.

66. A noble gas (or inert gas) is a highly unreactive element with a full valence shell.

67. A halogen is a highly reactive element needing one electron to fill its valence shell.

68. An orbital refers to the allowed energy state of an electron in an atom based on its principal, orbital, and magnetic quantum numbers.

69. Diagnosis refers to identifying a condition, disease, or disorder. Prognosis is a prediction for how it will develop and the outcome after treatment is given.

70. Stress is an exerted force per cross-sectional unit of area. Strain is a measure of the degree to which an object deforms as a result of the stress.

71. Hemoglobin is the protein in red blood cells which transports oxygen.

72. A genome is all of the genetic information found in the DNA of an organism.

73. An object is submerged when it is placed below the surface of a liquid.

74. Benign is non-cancerous, while malignant is cancerous.

75. A transistor is a semiconductor device that can act as a switch or an amplifier.

76. Leukemia refers to cancer of blood-forming cells and tissues, including bone marrow.

77. A polar molecule has a dipole moment; it can be divided (by an imaginary line) in such a way as to be positive on one side and negative on the other side.

78. A lesion refers to an injury or an abnormal change in tissue.

79. Torque equals force times lever arm and causes a rigid body to develop angular acceleration.

80. A free radical has one or more unpaired electrons.

81. A capacitor is a device that stores charge, consisting of two separated conductors.

82. An antigen is a toxin or potentially harmful substance that triggers an immune response from the body, which entails producing an antibody to neutralize it.

83. Acute means abrupt onset and severe. For a symptom like pain, the duration is usually short. For a disease, it may also mean rapidly progressing.

84. A biome is a group of ecosystems that share similar climates and have organisms with similar characteristics.

85. Ozone is the O_3 allotrope of oxygen. (The most common allotrope, O_2, forms at STP). The ozone layer is a layer of the stratosphere with a high concentration of ozone. It absorbs dangerous UV radiation from the sun.

86. Aqueous refers to a solution where the solvent is water.

87. In vertebrates, the abdomen lies between the thorax and pelvis, containing the digestive organs (and more), and is also known as the belly. In arthropods, the ab-

domen lies at the posterior, and contains reproductive organs (and more).

88. An electrolyte is a solute which produces ions in a solution.

89. Heterozygous refers to a plant or animal with two different alleles located at the same position on a chromosome. For homozygous, the alleles are the same.

90. Fission is a nuclear reaction where one nucleus splits into smaller nuclei. Fusion is a nuclear reaction where smaller nuclei are joined to form a heavier nucleus.

91. An organelle is a discrete cell structure that has a specialized function.

92. Wavelength is the distance that a wave travels in one cycle. Period is the time it takes to complete one oscillation. Frequency is the number of cycles per unit time.

93. An equinox refers to the two days of the year when the sun is at a position along the ecliptic that intersects the celestial equator, causing the day and night to be approximately equal in length. (Day and night aren't exactly equal on these two days due to atmospheric refraction and the finite size of the sun.) Vernal and autumnal are the two types of equinoxes.

94. A carbohydrate is a type of organic compound that typically has a chemical formula of the form $C_m(H_2O)_n$, where m and n are integers, and is a major nutrient in animal diets.

95. Cytoplasm refers to the protoplasm of a cell, excluding the nucleus (if it has one).

96. Ribosomes are cell organelles – present throughout the cytoplasm of a cell – consisting of RNA and proteins, where proteins are synthesized.

97. Boiling is a phase transition from liquid to gas. In evaporation, the fastest molecules escape from the liquid in vapor form without a phase change. Boiling occurs at the boiling point, whereas evaporation occurs even at temperatures much lower than the boiling point. Boiling occurs throughout the volume, whereas evaporation occurs at the surface of the liquid.

98. A nebula is an interstellar region consisting of dust or gas.

99. A pathogen is a disease-carrying agent, perhaps in the form of a microorganism.

100. Energy represents the ability to do work. Kinetic energy is work that can be done by changing speed. Potential energy is work that can be done by changing position. Activation energy is the energy needed for a reaction to occur.

101. Entropy provides a measure of the statistical disorder of the molecules of a substance.

102. The enthalpy of a system equals internal energy plus pressure times volume, where PV may be thought of as energy stored in the surroundings. For a reaction that occurs at constant pressure, the change in enthalpy equals the heat exchanged.

103. Niacin, also known as vitamin B3, is an essential vitamin in many common foods that helps humans keep their nervous system, digestive system, and skin healthy.

104. In geology, a delta refers to the sediment that accumulates (often in the shape of a triangle) where the mouth of a river meets a large body of water.

105. A buffer is an aqueous solution that can neutralize an acid or base added in a small amount (such that the pH level doesn't change appreciably).

106. A confounding variable is a factor other than the independent variable being manipulated which may affect the outcome of an experiment.

107. A black hole is a celestial object (such as a collapsed star) with so much mass that its gravitational field prevents even light from escaping.

108. A lattice is a three-dimensional array of atoms (or groups of atoms).

109. Pressure is force per unit area. For a fluid, this is equivalent to density times gravitational acceleration times depth. Buoyancy refers to the net upward pressure (which results in a buoyant force) exerted on an object submerged in a fluid (as a result of greater upward pressure at the bottom of the object compared to smaller downward pressure at the top of the object, due to variation of pressure with depth).

110. Solubility at a given temperature is the amount of solute needed to dissolve in

a given amount of solvent in order for the solution to be saturated.

111. A tendon is tough connective tissue joining skeletal muscles to bones.

112. A clavicle is the collarbone.

113. Linear momentum, also called momentum, equals mass times velocity. Angular momentum is an analogous form of momentum for a rotating object, which equals moment of inertia times angular velocity.

114. Cellulose is the main constituent of the walls of plant cells

115. Excretion is the process by which an organism eliminates metabolic wastes.

116. Oncology is the branch of medicine that studies the diagnosis and treatment of cancer.

117. Refraction refers to the bending of a ray of light as it passes from one medium to another medium (in which light travels a different speed).

118. Diffraction refers to the bending of light around an obstacle, such as when it passes through a narrow slit (or through a grating).

119. Dispersion refers to the separation of light into its constituent colors.

120. Kinesthesis is the system for sensing the position, orientation, movement, etc. of the different parts of the body.

121. Chlorophyll is the green pigment found in plant cells, and is essential for photo-synthesis.

122. A subduction zone refers to the sinking of one lithospheric plate under another when two lithospheric plates collide.

123. The umbra is the portion of the shadow of an eclipse where sunlight can't be seen. The penumbra is the portion of the shadow of an eclipse where sunlight shows partially. (Alternatively, these terms may also be used to describe sunspots.)

124. The epidermis is the outer layer of the skin. The dermis lies beneath it.

125. Right ascension is celestial longitude. Declination is celestial latitude.

126. In health science, a contusion is a more technical term for bruise.

127. Glacial striations are grooves and scratches that form during glacial abrasion.

128. A dielectric is a non-conducting material that can sustain an electric field. A capacitor can store more charge when it includes a dielectric between its plates.

129. Beta carotene is a reddish-orange pigment found in many fruits and vegetables, which the human body converts into vitamin A.

130. Fungi, which include mold, mildew, mushrooms, and yeast, usually have chitin in their cell walls, are usually immobile, are often parasites, and often feed by decomposing organic matter.

131. Isotropy refers to a property that is the same in all directions.

132. Glucose has the chemical formula $C_6H_{12}O_6$ and is the main sugar found in blood.

133. In geology, a basin is a wide, rounded depression in which the rock layers incline toward a spot near the center.

134. Action potential is a neural impulse.

135. Remission is when the symptoms of a disease disappear or lessen.

136. A process that requires oxygen is aerobic, whereas a process that does not require oxygen is anaerobic.

137. Aerobic exercise increases the efficiency with which the body takes in oxygen, increasing the fitness of the heart and lungs.

138. A macroscopic collision is elastic if mechanical energy is conserved, inelastic if mechanical energy isn't conserved, and perfectly inelastic if the objects stick together. (A collision between two point-like particles is elastic if identical particles appear in both the initial and final states, and is inelastic otherwise; for a collision between point-like particles, energy is conserved by the system.) Note that the law of conservation of momentum may apply regardless of whether a collision is elastic.

139. In a longitudinal wave, the amplitude of oscillation is aligned with the direction

of propagation. In a transverse wave, the amplitude of oscillation is perpendicular to the direction of propagation.

140. Resonance is the phenomenon where the frequency is just right such that the reflected waves create a standing wave with a much larger amplitude than any of the individual waves.

141. Larynx is the technical term for voice box.

142. The Kuiper Belt is a large belt of icy bodies in the outer solar system, which is the source of many comets and some dwarf planets like Pluto. The Oort Cloud is a vast spherical shell extending beyond the Kuiper Belt, which also contains icy bodies.

143. A tumor is an abnormal mass of tissue growth. It is not necessarily cancerous.

144. A calorimeter is a device that measures the amount of heat exchanged. A simple calorimeter consists of a container of liquid with a thermometer, to which another substance (of different temperature than the liquid) may be added.

145. Agriculture is the branch of science that studies farming.

146. A colloid is a mixture where particles dispersed throughout remain suspended in the medium. (The term may refer to such particles or to the entire mixture.)

147. A shock wave results when an object travels faster than the speed of the waves it produces in a medium. Examples include V-shaped waves that ducks and boats create in water and the sonic boom created by supersonic aircraft.

148. Pneumonia refers to an infection that inflames the alveoli of the lungs.

149. In geology, strata are layers of sedimentary rock.

150. A quark is a subatomic particle with fractional charge always found in groups of two or three. They make up baryons (like the proton and neutron) and mesons (like the pion and kaon). The six flavors include up, down, charm, strange, top, and bottom (not to be confused with colors, which are red, green, and blue).

151. Mitochondria are cell organelles that generate ATP (a source of chemical energy).

152. A photon is a single particle of light corresponding to one quantum of energy.

153. A helium nucleus is released during alpha decay, an electron or positron is released during beta decay, and a photon is released during gamma decay.

154. An acid is a substance that increases the concentration of H^+ (aq) when it dissolves in water. A base is a substance that increases the concentration of OH^- (aq) when it dissolves in water.

155. Glaucoma is a group of eye conditions featuring increased pressure and nerve damage, which can lead to blindness.

156. Melanin is a dark brown pigment in skin that absorbs UV rays.

157. Cryogenics is the branch of science that studies low-temperature physics.

158. A crystalline solid features a regular geometric arrangement of its molecules, atoms, or ions.

159. An amorphous solid lacks the regular geometric pattern of crystalline solids.

160. Chloroplast is a cell organelle in plants and green algae where photosynthesis occurs.

161. Eukaryotes are organisms with cells that contain a nucleus and prokaryotes are unicellular organisms (such as bacteria) with cells that don't contain a nucleus.

162. An aperture is a small opening (or its diameter) through which light enters to pass through the lens of a camera, telescope, or other optical instrument.

163. Hyperglycemia is abnormally high blood sugar and hypoglycemia is abnormally low blood sugar (in terms of concentration).

164. Oxidation is a reaction where a substance loses electrons. Reduction is a reaction where a substance gains electrons. (Since an electron is negative, its charge is reduced.)

165. A cation is an ion with positive charge. An anion is an ion with negative charge.

166. A cathode is an electrode where reduction occurs. An anode is an electrode where oxidation occurs.

167. Basalt is a dark, fine-grained igneous rock that is rich in magnesium and iron, and is low in silica content.

168. Adrenal glands are a pair of endocrine organs above the kidney. They secrete hormones that help with metabolism, immunity, stress, etc.

169. A positron is the antiparticle of the electron. It has the same mass as an electron, but is positively charged.

170. An estuary is a wetland that forms where a river meets an ocean.

171. The cornea is the tough transparent tissue that covers the iris and pupil of the eye.

172. The cochlea is the spiraling part of the inner ear where sound is detected.

173. Biotic factors refer to living (or previously living) elements and abiotic factors refer to non-living elements.

174. Autism is a disorder characterized by communication difficulties and impaired social interaction, which appears during childhood.

175. A stalactite (think "t" for top or "c" for ceiling) is a mineral deposit resembling an icicle which hangs from the roof of a cave. A stalagmite (think "g" for ground) is a cone-shaped mineral deposit rising up from the floor of a cave.

176. Two (or more) isomers of the same compound have the same chemical composition, but different structures.

177. A transformer is a device consisting of primary and secondary coils of wire, which applies Faraday's law in order to step AC voltage up or down.

178. Flux could be the rate of flow of a quantity across a surface, or it could be a measure of the number of field lines passing through a surface. Types of flux include electric flux, magnetic flux, gravitational flux, energy flux, momentum flux, heat flux, mass flux, diffusion flux, particle flux, probability flux density, Poynting flux, and the list goes on. You should have named electric, magnetic, and at least 1-2 others.

179. Viscosity provides a measure of internal friction in the flow of a fluid.

180. In an emergency room or on a battlefield, triage refers to assigning priority to patients based on factors like severity of wounds and prospects for survival.

181. Riboflavin, also known as vitamin B2, is important for the growth and function of cells.

182. A bolometer measures the power of electromagnetic radiation. It is useful, for example, in astronomy for wavelengths from a submillimeter to the far infrared.

183. Retrograde motion refers to a short period for which a planet appears to travel backward relative to the stars as viewed from earth compared to the direction that it normally appears to travel relative to the stars. Bonus if you can explain why.

184. Salmonella infection is a bacterial disease commonly caused by contaminated food or water, which affects the intestines.

185. Simple harmonic motion is sinusoidal motion experienced when the net force on an object is proportional to the negative of the displacement of the object from equilibrium (for example, when the net force equals the restoring force exerted by a spring), in which case the acceleration is also proportional to the negative of the displacement of the object from equilibrium.

186. Propagate refers to the traveling of a wave, often with the sense of spreading outward (like a ripple in water or like a sound wave), but it could just mean to transmit through a medium (like a ray of light traveling through glass).

187. Adiabatic refers to a process that occurs without any heat exchange.

188. In geology, ablation refers to material (ice and snow) lost by a glacier (or the amount of this lost material that is melted).

189. Propulsion refers to the act of propelling, pushing, or driving an object forward, such as to accelerate an object (but such a system is also necessary to overcome resistive forces like air resistance just to maintain constant velocity in an atmosphere). Thrust is a driving force that generates propulsion. Thrust is created from Newton's

third law: By ejecting a fluid backwards, for example, Newton's third law produces an equal and opposite reactionary force of thrust on a rocket.

190. A cosmic ray is a stream of high-energy particles (such as protons or helium nuclei) from space which interact with atoms in earth's atmosphere.

191. A polymer is a giant molecule which consists of monomers chained together.

192. Coniferous trees produce cones and have needle-like leaves. Deciduous trees shed their leaves annually.

193. A hadron is a particle composed of quarks, such as a baryon (three quarks) or a meson (quark-antiquark pair).

194. A lepton is a fermion that isn't subject to the strong nuclear force, and includes the electron, muon, tau particle, and their neutrinos.

195. Isostasy is basically the concept of buoyancy applied to earth's crust, that it is "floating" in equilibrium (with balanced pressures) on the mantle.

196. Mitosis refers to the division of the nucleus of a eukaryotic cell. Phases include prophase, metaphase, anaphase, and telophase.

197. A heat engine is a device that adapts the natural flow of heat from a thermal reservoir at high temperature to a thermal reservoir at low temperature in order to perform mechanical work.

198. Dendrites extend from neurons and carry impulses.

199. Moment of inertia provides a measure of a rigid body's tendency to maintain constant angular momentum (which is a sense of rotational inertia).

200. The thalamus is the gray matter in the brain which receives sensory messages and relays them to parts of the cerebrum. The hypothalamus lies under the thalamus and regulates basic body functions like hunger, fatigue, and body temperature.

201. A solenoid is a coil of wire in the shape of a right-circular cylinder, which serves as a magnet when carrying current (and may or may not have an iron core).

202. Pumice is porous volcanic rock, which is typically light in color and less dense than water.

203. A thermal reservoir is a heat source that offers (or may receive) a virtually limitless supply of thermal energy, with virtually no effect on the temperature of the heat source.

204. Hepatitis is inflammation of the liver. Bonus if you can describe A, B, and C.

205. The Gregorian calendar (currently in use) has 365 days in most years, a 366th day on years divisible by 4 (called leap year) but not years divisible by 100 (unless they are also divisible by 400). For example, 2000 had a leap year because it was divisible by 400, but 2100 won't have a leap year, whereas 2104, 2108, 2112, etc. will have leap years. The Julian calendar (used previously) has 365 days in most years and a 366th day on years divisible by 4 without any exceptions. The problem with the Julian calendar is that one astronomical year is slightly shorter than 365.25 days long, and the Gregorian calendar corrects for this discrepancy.

206. A vestigial structure is a trait inherited from an ancestor which has lost most or all of its original function, like the appendix in humans.

207. Impulse equals the change in an object's momentum or, equivalently, the product of the average collision force and the time duration of the collision.

208. Luminosity is the total amount of energy radiated or emitted per unit time. It is equivalent to the radiant power. For a star, luminosity provides a measure of its intrinsic brightness (which we can use to determine its apparent brightness from earth).

209. A pheromone is a chemical substance secreted by an animal, which impacts the behavior of other animals in the same species.

210. An eddy current is induced in a metal that travels through a magnetic field (by Faraday's law), which is often undesirable from a practical perspective because this dissipates energy (in the form of heat).

211. A polypeptide is a long chain of amino acids. Polypeptides are found in proteins.

212. Atwood's machine consists of two masses connected to a cord that passes over a pulley, which is suspended in the air. When the system is released from rest, the heavier mass falls down, pulling the lighter mass upward. Atwood's machine is useful for measuring gravitational field (since it involves long time durations compared to dropping an object from rest).

213. Orthopedic surgeons specialize in disorders relating to the musculoskeletal system, including bones, joints, tendons, etc.

214. An ideal gas has sufficiently low density so as to obey the law PV = nRT. Bonus for describing an ideal gas at the molecular level, such as assuming identical molecules, negligible intermolecular forces (except for collisions), momentum and kinetic energy are conserved for collisions, motions are random, molecules obey Newton's laws of motion, and there are very many molecules with large separations.

215. Pneumatics is the branch of engineering that studies compressed gases.

216. Entomology is the branch of zoology that studies insects.

217. Stoichiometry is the branch of chemistry that studies the quantitative relationships between reactants and products in reactions.

218. On a standing wave, a node is a point that does not oscillate and an anti-node is a point where there is maximum oscillation.

219. An insulator (**not** inductor) is the opposite of a conductor.

220. An inductor is a coil of conducting wire (or even a single loop of wire), such that Faraday's law applies to it.

221. An endoplasmic reticulum is a network of membranes in the cytoplasm of a eukaryotic cell, which is involved in the synthesis of proteins and lipids.

222. Duality means that light exhibits both wave-like and particle-like properties, and also means that a "particle" like an electron also exhibits wave-like properties

(the latter is according to the de Broglie relation).

223. In astronomy, libration refers to the oscillation of an object around a stable point in the three-body problem. In the sun-earth-moon problem, this results in a slight wobble of the moon in its orbit around earth, allowing us to see a little more than 50% of its surface (which would be expected since the moon always shows the same side toward the earth due to tidal lock).

224. In astronomy, precession refers to a slight change in the position of the stars as viewed from earth due to the tilt of earth's axis.

225. Dark matter is non-luminous matter in the universe that can't be seen through a telescope, but which is postulated to exist to explain gravitational effects that can't be explained solely from visible matter.

226. Metacarpals are the five bones in each hand connecting the fingers to the wrists.

227. In a basic sense, orthogonal means perpendicular. (Bonus if you can do better.)

228. A neutrino is a neutral particle with very little mass, which interacts only very weakly with other particles (and through the weak nuclear force).

229. Ventral refers to the region of the body near the belly, dorsal refers to the back side, and lateral means toward the side.

230. The Carnot cycle has the maximum possible efficiency for a heat engine that operates between a given pair of high and low temperatures.

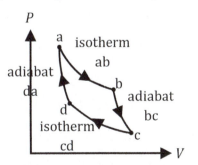

231. Nucleosynthesis refers to the formation of the heavier elements, which occurs in stars.

232. The polarization of a beam of light occurs when the electric fields of all of the waves in the beam oscillate in a common direction. Light may be polarized by reflection (maximized for Brewster's angle), passing through a birefringent crystal (like calcite), through scattering, or by passing through a polarizer.

233. Arrhythmia is an irregularity in the beating of the heart.

234. A cyclotron is a particle accelerator in the shape of a circle.

235. In biology, an axon is a long fiber that carries an impulse away from a neuron.

236. A nephron is a structure in the kidneys which collects waste (in the form of urine) and purifies blood.

237. Ebola is an RNA virus which causes fever and internal bleeding, often resulting in death.

238. The work function of a metal is the minimum energy with which an electron is bound to its atoms.

239. Embolism refers to a foreign material (like a blood clot) that obstructs a blood vessel.

240. Pair production occurs when two photons produce an electron and positron, $\gamma + \gamma \rightarrow e^- + e^+$, and pair annihilation is the opposite, $e^- + e^+ \rightarrow \gamma + \gamma$.

241. Graphene is an allotrope of carbon in a hexagonal lattice just one atom thick, yet is very strong. (Andre Geim and Konstantin Novoselov received a Nobel Prize in 2010 for their research on graphene.)

242. In quantum mechanics, normalizing a wave function is a method to determine an unknown coefficient by demanding that there be 100% probability of finding the particle somewhere, using an integral (in 1D) of the form $\int_{x=-\infty}^{\infty} \psi^* \psi \, dx = 1$.

243. Stem cells are unspecialized cells found in adults, which replicate to produce new body tissues, becoming specialized cells in the process.

244. The ancient Greeks devised (an incorrect) geocentric model with the earth at

the center of the solar system, which used epicycles and deferents. The deferent is a large circle centered around the earth, and the epicycle is a smaller circle containing a planet (such as Mars). The epicycle rotates as it travels along the deferent. (This forms a curve known as the epicycloid in geometry.) The Greeks improved on this idea by placing the earth not at the exact center of the deferent, but by placing the earth a little off-center, equally distant from a symmetric point called the equant. The epicycle revolved around the equant with uniform angular speed.

245. Phlogiston was a hypothetical substance thought to be involved in burning, but now we know that combustion occurs without any such substance.

246. A Hertzsprung-Russell diagram plots luminosity (or, equivalently, absolute magnitude) on the vertical axis and spectral type (or, equivalently, color, wavelength, or temperature) on the horizontal axis for stars. Most of the stars in the night sky appear on a diagonal known as the main sequence. The H-R diagram illustrates the life cycle of a star and can be used to determine the distance from earth to a galaxy.

247. Meningitis refers to inflammation of the membranes (known as the meninges) that enclose the central nervous system, usually caused by infection.

248. A synapse is the junction between a neuron and an adjacent cell, allowing an impulse to be transferred.

249. Magnetic hysteresis refers to a lag in the magnetization of a ferromagnetic material when the magnetizing force varies, such that if the magnetizing force increases and then decreases to its original value, a plot of the magnetization as a function of the magnetizing force includes a loop (rather than simply retracing the curve).

250. The gall bladder stores bile until food enters the small intestine.

251. The ether was a hypothetical substance once believed to fill space, thought to serve as a medium for the transmission of light waves. The Michelson-Morley experiment failed to support the ether theory.

3 Who's That Scientist?

1. Claudius Ptolemy, Aristotle, and Hipparchus (favored the geocentric model)

2. Galileo Galilei (made extensive use of the telescope in the early 1600's)

3. Niels Bohr (proposed a quantum model of the hydrogen atom)

4. Archimedes (discovered buoyancy)

5. Albert Einstein (presented an explanation for the photoelectric effect)

6. Benjamin Franklin (described charges as "positive" and "negative")

7. Eratosthenes (calculated the circumference of the earth)

8. Marie Curie (received one Nobel Prize in physics and another in chemistry)

9. Charles Coulomb (has an inverse-square law that now bears his name)

10. Johannes Kepler (deduced that planets travel in elliptical orbits)

11. Sir Isaac Newton (wrote the *Principia*)

12. Ernest Rutherford (discovered the positively charged nucleus)

13. Nikola Tesla (played a significant role in developing AC electricity)

14. Neil Armstrong and Buzz Aldrin (landed on the moon on July 20, 1969); note that Michael Collins was orbiting in the command module at this time

15. Nicolaus Copernicus (revived the heliocentric model)

16. Leucippus, Democritus, and Epicurus (proposed atomic views)

17. Sir Francis Bacon (is credited with developing the scientific method)

18. Alexander Graham Bell (invented the telephone)

19. John Dalton (is known for introducing atomic theory in the early 1800's)

20. Orville and Wilbur Wright (are credited with the first successful airplane flight)

21. Stephen Hawking (predicted that black holes emit radiation)

22. Thomas Alva Edison (invented the phonograph)

23. Hippocrates II (credited with the Hippocratic Oath)

24. Charles Darwin (published *On the Origin of Species*)

25. Louis Pasteur (developed a technique that now bears his name)

26. Robert Hooke (coined the term "cell" and discovered Hooke's law)

27. James Hutton (published *Theory of the Earth*)

28. Jean-Baptiste Lamarck (coined the term "invertebrates")

29. Gregor Johann Mendel (coined the terms "dominant" and "recessive")

30. Charles Richter (devised a magnitude scale for measuring seismic activity)

31. Tim Berners-Lee (invented the world wide web)

32. Sigmund Freud (published *The Interpretation of Dreams* on psychoanalysis)

33. Isaac Asimov (was a prolific writer of science fiction and popular science); note that Karel Čapek introduced the word "robot" in 1920, while Isaac Asimov made the natural leap from "robot" to the field of "robotics"

34. Edward Jenner (pioneered the smallpox vaccine)

35. Lord Kelvin nee William Thomson (proposed an absolute scale of temperature)

36. Brian Randolph Greene (popularized string theory with *The Fabric of the Cosmos*)

37. René Laennec (invented the stethoscope)

38. Carl Linnaeus (is credited with developing binomial nomenclature)

39. James Prescott Joule (showed that heat is a form of energy)

40. Alexander Fleming, Howard Flory, and Ernst Chain (discovered penicillin)

41. Dmitri Mendeleev and Lothar Meyer (contributed towards the periodic table)

42. Frederick Griffith (reported on bacterial transformation)

43. Oswald Avery, Collin MacLeod, and Maclyn McCarty (isolated DNA, and not protein as believed at the time, as the carrier of genetic information)

44. James Dewey Watson and Francis Crick (discovered the structure of DNA)

45. Sir Joseph John Thomson (discovered the electron)

46. Edwin Hubble (discovered galaxies comparable in size to the Milky Way)

47. Thomas Hunt Morgan (studied the role that chromosomes play in heredity)

48. Carl Sagan (wrote *Contact* and promoted SETI)

49. Werner Heisenberg (developed an uncertainty principle that now bears his name)

50. Amedeo Avogadro (proposed the hypothesis that now bears his name); note that Joseph Louis Gay-Lussac's law is quite similar

51. Thomas Young (performed the double-slit experiment)

52. Antonie van Leeuernhoek, aka Anton (made extensive early use of microscopes)

53. Erwin Schrodinger (developed a wave equation for quantum mechanics)

54. Aristarchus (proposed a heliocentric model for the solar system)

55. Blaise Pascal (has an SI unit and a programming language named after him)

56. Michael Faraday (discovered the induction law that now bears his name)

57. Alfred Russel Wallace (described natural selection independently of Darwin)

58. Louis de Broglie (discovered the wave-like properties of electrons)

59. Johannes van der Waals (introduced a formula for more realistic gases)

60. Ole Roemer (estimated the speed of light in 1676)

61. Wolfgang Pauli (formulated the exclusion principle that now bears his name)

62. Robert A. Millikan (measured the charge of an electron)

63. Max Planck (showed that energy is quantized)

64. Willard Libby (developed radioactive carbon dating)

65. Joseph Leonard Goldstein and Michael Brown (received a Nobel Prize for their work on cholesterol)

66. Hipparchus (discovered the precession of the equinoxes)

67. James Clerk Maxwell (is credited with assembling the set of four equations that now bears his name)

68. Harry Hess and Robert Dietz (independently wrote about seafloor spreading in the early 1960's); note that Arthur Holmes mentioned the idea in a textbook in 1944

69. Henry Cavendish (produced hydrogen and measured the gravitational constant)

70. James Chadwick (discovered the neutron)

71. Martinus Beijerinck (coined the term "virus")

72. Wilhelm Maximilian Wundt (is credited with founding the first psychology lab)

73. Alfred Wegener (suggested the ideas of the Pangaea and continental drift); note that Sir Francis Bacon had hinted at the notion in 1620, and F.B. Taylor outlined the idea of continental drift in a paper two years before Wegener

74. Hendrik A. Lorentz and Pieter Zeeman (for their work on the Zeeman effect)

75. Rachel Carson (wrote *Silent Spring*)

76. Walther Nernst (formulated the third law of thermodynamics)

77. Pierre Paul Broca, aka Paul Broca (discovered the area of the brain that now bears his name)

78. Allen and Beatrix Gardner (trained a chimpanzee in American sign language)

79. Ian Wilmut (is credited for leading a research group that cloned a sheep)

80. Antoine Lavoisier (is considered by some to be the father of modern chemistry)

81. Albert Abraham Michelson and Edward Williams Morley (set out to detect small changes in the speed of light, but failed to detect any such changes)

82. Gilbert Newton Lewis (introduced structures that now bear his name)

83. Hermann Rorschach (created the inkblot test that now bears his name)

84. Joseph Edward Murray and Edward Donnall Thomas (worked on transplants)

85. Nicolaus Steno, aka Nicolas (introduced the law of superposition in the 1600's)

86. Roger Wolcott Sperry (studied split-brain patients)

87. Sheldon L. Glashow, Abdus Salam, and Steven Weinberg (the standard model)

88. Eugene Aserinski and Nathaniel Kleitman (described rapid eye movement)

89. Frederick Sanger (received Nobel Prizes in chemistry in 1958 and 1980)

90. John Bardeen (received Nobel Prizes in physics in 1956 and 1972)

4 Give an Example

If you name fewer items than requested, you should award yourself partial credit. For example, if a question asks for 4 items, listing 3 correctly merits 3/4 credit.

1. Energy: potential energy (or specific kinds, like gravitational and spring), kinetic energy (including rotational), activation energy, ionization energy, heat energy (or specifically endothermic and exothermic) or thermal energy, ground state energy, binding energy, wind energy, solar energy, Gibbs free energy, mechanical energy, vibrational energy, zero-point energy, Fermi energy, relativistic energy, nonconservative work (energy lost to friction, air drag, etc.), and the list goes on.

2. Physical changes: thermal expansion, evaporation, any phase transition (such as boiling or freezing), crumpling paper, magnetizing iron, cutting cardboard, etc.

3. Chemical changes: you just need to mention or describe one of numerous chemical reactions, like combustion, the hydrolysis of water, rusting of iron, forming salt, etc.

4. Amphibians: frogs and toads, salamanders and newts, and caecilian.

5. Forces: weight (but **not** mass), tension, friction, normal force, air drag, restoring force (or spring force), centripetal force, centrifugal force, electric force, magnetic force, Lorentz force, buoyant force, drive force, net force, strong and weak nuclear forces, etc. (but **not** speed, acceleration, torque, impulse, or other quantities where the SI unit isn't a Newton).

6. Mineral species: quartz, calcite, pyrite, opal, topaz, talc, amethyst, feldspar, etc. (but **not** pure elements like copper, silver, etc., including forms of carbon like diamond or graphite). Note that silicates, carbonates, oxides, etc. are classes, **not** species.

7. Nonrenewable resources: fossil fuels (including crude oil, natural gas, and coal; okay to list separately), nuclear fuels (like uranium), minerals, metal ores, etc.

8. Renewable resources: solar energy, wind, water (but with exceptions), timber, geothermal energy, biomass, etc.

9. Viable sources of error: air resistance (if there is motion), rotational inertia (if there are wheels), limited precision of the measuring device (but only if the device tolerance is significant compared to the percent error), approximation made in the theory (assuming an ideal gas, for example), non-uniformity of the material used, calibration issues (especially, if you took time to substantiate this during lab), etc.

10. Problematic sources of error: round-off error (avoidable by keeping additional digits and only rounding the final answer), calculator error (seldom are more digits needed than a calculator provides), bumping the apparatus (simply redo the measurement), procedural mistakes (pay better attention or repeat the experiment), parallax error (you can avoid it), human error (it's okay for the error to be human in origin, but this term is way too broad; be specific), equipment malfunction (get it fixed and it won't impact the results), partners or the TA weren't helpful (could be true, but it probably won't get you points to mention it), hypothetical statements (better to base your idea on something that you actually observed during the lab), etc.

11. Chemistry lab attire: wear safety goggles or glasses, wear a lab coat, wear a shirt that covers the belly, wear pants that cover the knees and lower legs, wear shoes that cover the feet completely, keep hair from blocking the eyes, clothing should not hang loosely (ties, scarves, straps, etc.), etc.

12. Galaxies: Milky Way, Andromeda, Cygnus A, Magellanic Clouds, Whirlpool, Sombrero, Cartwheel, Centaurus A, Antennae, Cigar, etc.

13. Moons of Earth: Luna (or "the moon"). Moons of Mars: Phobos, Deimos.

Moons of Jupiter: Ganymede, Callisto, Io, Europa, Himalia, Amalthea, Thebe, etc.

Moons of Saturn: Titan, Rhea, Lapetus, Dione, Tethys, Enceladus, Hyperion, etc.

Moons of Uranus: Titania, Oberon, Umbriel, Ariel, Miranda, etc.

Moons of Neptune: Triton, etc. (As a dwarf planet, Pluto's moons don't count.)

14. Convex meniscus: mercury is the main answer.

15. Inverse-square laws: Newton's law of gravity, Coulomb's law (or Gauss's law), the intensity of light radiated from a star, pressure of sound radiated from a point source in air.

16. Important cycles in science: water, cell, rock, oxygen, nitrogen, carbon, recycling, thermodynamic (Carnot, Otto, etc.), etc.

17. Cell organelle functions: store materials (vacuoles), protection (wall), division (centrioles), control center (nucleus), breakdown (lysosomes), synthesize proteins (ribosomes), transport (endoplasmic reticulum), convert solar energy to chemical energy (chloroplasts), convert chemical energy (mitochondria), package (Golgi), etc.

18. Forms of carbon: diamond, graphite, charcoal, graphene, carbon nanotube, etc.

19. Measuring devices: scale (weight), stopwatch (time), thermometer (temperature), graduated cylinder (volume), meterstick (length), protractor (angle), litmus test (pH), Vernier calipers (length), micrometer (length), calorimeter (heat), compass (earth's magnetic field), ammeter (current), voltmeter (potential difference), electroscope (charge), mass spectrometer (chemical composition), photogate (speed), etc.

20. m or M: mass (m), meter (m, as a unit), milli (m, as a prefix), mega (M, as a prefix), molarity (M), molality (m), magnetization (M), etc.

21. Vectors: velocity, displacement (or directed distance), acceleration, force, weight, momentum, angular momentum, angular velocity, torque, electric field, magnetic field, current density, etc.

22. Scalars: speed, time, length, mass, work, energy, power, angular speed, period, wavelength, frequency, charge, capacitance, electric potential, inductance, flux, etc. (We will accept moment of inertia, though it is technically a second-rank tensor.)

23. Baby farm animals: chick (chicken), foal, colt, filly (horse), calf (cow), piglet (pig), lamb (sheep), kid (goat), gosling (goose), etc.

24. Engineering: mechanical, industrial, electrical, civil, structural, software, chemical,

biomedical, aerospace, metallurgy, etc.

25. Less dense than water: hydrogen, helium, air, wood, ice, oxygen, nitrogen, carbon dioxide, lithium, ammonia, benzene, etc. (especially gases).

26. Strong acids: H_2SO_4, HNO_3, HCl, HI, $HClO_3$, $HClO_4$, HBr, etc.

27. Strong bases: $NaOH$, $Ba(OH)_2$, KOH, $Ca(OH)_2$, $LiOH$, etc.

28. Digestive enzymes: Amylase, lactase, sucrase, pepsin, trypsin, lipase, maltase, etc.

29. Mostly transverse: ripples in water, electromagnetic wave, pulse along a string, S wave in seismology, etc.

30. Mostly longitudinal: sound wave, a wave traveling along the axis of a spring, P wave in seismology, etc.

31. Alkali metals: lithium, sodium, potassium, rubidium, cesium, and francium.

32. Dwarf planets: Pluto, Ceres, and Eris. We'll accept Makemake and Haumea.

33. Diatomic gases: H_2, N_2, O_2, F_2, Cl_2 (and Br_2 and I_2, but these aren't gases at STP).

34. Metamorphosis: butterfly, frog/toad, beetle, salamander, grasshopper, etc.

35. Bacterial diseases: tuberculosis, tetanus, cholera, leprosy, meningitis, diphtheria, streptococcus, Lyme disease, salmonellosis, whooping cough, etc.

36. Viral diseases: common cold, influenza, chicken pox, smallpox, measles, warts, hepatitis B, rabies, mumps, polio, West Nile Virus, HIV, Ebola, rubella, etc.

37. Covalent/molecular: H_2, H_2O, CO, CO_2, CH_4, NH_3, NO, NO_2, O_2, SO_2, HCl, etc.

38. Ionic: $NaCl$, $MgCl_2$, LiF, MgO, $CaCl_2$, K_2S, Fe_2O_3, $CuCl_2$, Na_2O, BaS, $CuSO_4$, etc.

39. Mechanical weathering: frost wedging, sheeting, salt crystal growth, thermal expansion, plant roots, burrowing animals. Chemical weathering: oxidation, hydrolysis, dissolution, spheroidal. We'll also accept differential weathering.

40. Polar liquids: water, ammonia, ethanol, methanol, hydrochloric acid, etc.

41. Nonpolar liquids: gasoline, fats, oil, turpentine, toluene, etc.

42. Fungi: mold, mildew, mushroom, yeast, chytrids, etc.

43. Protists: algae, amoeba, kelp, euglena, etc. We'll accept slime mold.

44. Organic compounds: methane, ethane, propane, butane, hexane, octane, ethanol, methanol, ester, ether, glucose, sucrose, cellulose, cholesterol, caffeine, acetic acid, etc.

45. Redox reactions: combustion, corrosion (such as the rusting of iron), metal displacement, photosynthesis, cellular respiration, electrochemical cells, etc.

46. Passive cell transport: diffusion, facilitated diffusion, osmosis.

Active cell transport: protein pumps, endocytosis, exocytosis.

47. Strong electrolytes: H_2SO_4, HNO_3, HCl, HI, $HClO_3$, $HClO_4$, HBr, NaOH, KOH, $Ba(OH)_2$, etc.

48. Psychological therapy: psychoanalysis, group, behavior, cognitive, family, self-help, operant conditioning, humanistic, exposure, psychotherapy, drug, etc.

49. Sublimation: dry ice (solid carbon dioxide), snow (to some extent in certain cases of direct sunlight), comets (passing near enough to the sun).

50. Sedimentary rock: limestone, sandstone, coal, chalk (form of limestone), shale, etc.

51. Non-electromagnetic radiation: cosmic radiation, alpha radiation (a form of nuclear radiation), beta radiation, neutron radiation, gravitational radiation, etc. (but **not** radio, microwaves, x-rays, gamma rays, IR, UV, which are electromagnetic).

52. Anxiety disorders: panic, phobia, obsessive-compulsive (OCD), post-traumatic stress (PTSD), and generalized are the five main kinds.

53. Gene mutations: point, substitution, insertion, deletion, frameshift, chromosomal, duplication, inversion, translocation.

54. Shapes of molecules (that aren't cubic): linear, bent, planar, trigonal, pyramid, bipyramidal, tetrahedral, octahedral, etc. (but **not** simple cubic, bcc, fcc).

55. Plate boundaries' features: fault, trench, ridge, mountain range, rift valley, etc.

56. Molecular crystals: dry ice, methane, ammonia, argon, etc.

57. Covalent crystals: diamond, quartz, graphite, silicon carbide, etc.

58. Ionic crystals: NaCl, KF, KCl, NaF, KI, etc.

59. Rain forests: Amazon, Congo, Daintree, Valdivian, Bosawas (Nicaragua), etc.

60. Observatories: Mauna Kea, Palomar, SoHO, Chacaltaya, Mt. Wilson, VLA, etc.

61. Thermodynamic processes where one variable is held constant: adiabatic (no heat exchange), isothermal (constant temperature), steady state (constant internal energy), isobaric (constant pressure), isentropic (constant entropy), etc.

62. Detritivores: earthworms, dung flies, dung beetles, slugs, millipedes, etc.

63. Doppler effect: police radar, echocardiogram, Doppler radar, redshift of stars, etc.

64. Faraday's law: electric generator, motor, induction cooktop, transformer, etc.

65. Spectroscopy: chemical composition, structure of molecules, properties of stars, nuclear magnetic resonance (NMR) spectroscopy, etc.

66. Electrochemical cells: 1.5-Volt, car, or rechargeable battery, fuel cell, etc.

67. Nuclear radiation: nuclear medicine, radiometric dating, nuclear energy (fission of uranium), hydrogen bomb (nuclear fusion), etc.

68. Genetic engineering: modified crops, growth hormones, gene therapy, developing vaccines, creating antibodies, etc.

69. Silicates: glass, ceramics, microchips, piezoelectricity, watches, etc.

5 What's That Law or Principle?

1. Boyle's law: If the temperature of a fixed amount of gas is constant, the volume and pressure are inversely proportional.

2. Charles's law: If the pressure of a fixed amount of gas is constant, the volume and temperature are directly proportional.

3. The ideal gas law is $PV = nRT$. If the temperature is constant and the amount of gas is fixed, $PV = $ const., meaning that $P = \frac{\text{const.}}{V}$ according Boyle's law. If the pressure is constant and the amount of gas is fixed, $V = $ const. $\times T$ according to Charles's law.

4. Capillary action: When a glass capillary (which is a tube with a narrow diameter) is placed in a liquid, the liquid rises up the tube until the forces of adhesion, cohesion, and gravity are balanced.

5. Periodic law: When the elements are arranged according to atomic number, some properties occur at regular (or periodic) intervals.

6. Law of reflection: When a beam of light is incident upon a smooth surface, the reflected ray travels symmetrically, with the angle of reflection equal to the angle of incidence (where each angle is measured from the normal).

7. Conservation of energy: The total energy of the system and its surroundings is constant. Energy is neither created nor destroyed, but may change form.

8. For a chemical reaction, conservation of energy leads to conservation of mass. (Mass isn't conserved in general, such as for nuclear reactions. An extreme example is when an electron and positron annihilate, producing photons with zero rest mass.)

9. Newton's first law (inertia): Objects tend to maintain constant momentum. (We'll accept constant velocity, but constant speed isn't as good.)

Newton's second law: The net force on an object equals its mass times acceleration.

Newton's third law: If A exerts a force on B, then B exerts a force on A that is equal in magnitude but opposite in direction. (There is an equal and opposite reaction to every action.)

10. Kepler's first law: Planets travel in elliptical orbits with the sun at one focus.

Kepler's second law: Planets sweep out equal areas in equal times.

Kepler's third law: The square of a planet's orbital period is proportional to the cube of the semimajor axis of its (elliptical) orbit.

11. First law of thermodynamics: The change in internal energy of a system (with constant mole numbers) equals the heat absorbed minus the work done.

Second law of thermodynamics: The total entropy of a system plus its surroundings can't decrease. Alternatively, a heat engine can't be perfectly efficient.

Third law of thermodynamics: It is impossible to reach exactly absolute zero.

Zeroth law of thermodynamics: If A and B are each in thermal equilibrium with C, then A and B are also in thermal equilibrium with each other.

12. Law of definite proportions: The ratio of the elements is always the same for a given pure compound. (The compound has a constant composition.)

13. Occam's razor: The simplest explanation (requiring the fewest assumptions) is generally preferable. (This is technically a principle of philosophy.)

14. Mendel's law of dominance: Alleles may be dominant or recessive. If there is at least one dominant allele, this allele gets used.

Mendel's law of segregation: The alleles for each gene segregate when a gamete forms.

Mendel's law of independent assortment: The segregation of alleles for one gene can be independent of the segregation of alleles for other genes.

15. Pascal's law: If the pressure applied to an enclosed liquid changes, that change in pressure is transmitted throughout the liquid (undiminished). This is why we add the atmospheric pressure, P_0, to $\rho g h$ to find the pressure in a fluid.

16. Pressure-flow hypothesis: Sap is transported in the phloem of plants from sources of sugar (like leaves) to regions with less sugar via pressure flow.

17. Avogadro's law: If gases with equal volumes have the same pressure and the same temperature, they will contain the same number of molecules.

18. Dalton's law of partial pressures: For a mixture of (non-reacting) gases, the total pressure of the mixture equals the sum of the pressures (called partial pressures) that each gas would exert (if it were the only gas).

19. Newton's law of gravity: Two masses attract one another with a gravitational force that is directly proportional to each mass and inversely proportional to the square of the separation between their centers.

20. Coulomb's law: Two charges attract or repel one another with an electric force that is directly proportional to each charge and inversely proportional to the square of the separation between their centers. The force is attractive for opposite charges and is repulsive for like charges.

21. One right-hand rule of magnetism relates current, magnetic field, and magnetic force. There is more than one equivalent way to formulate this right-hand rule. One way is to point the extended fingers of your right hand along the current, twist your forearm while still pointing the fingers along the current until you can naturally bend your fingers toward the magnetic field, and then your extended thumb will point along the magnetic force. We'll accept a (correctly) labeled diagram.

A second right-hand rule helps to determine the magnetic field lines created by a current. Wrap the fingers of your right hand along the wire with your thumb along the current. The curled fingers represent magnetic field "lines" circulating around the current (the fingernails indicate which way).

22. Ohm's law states that for a given conductor (which has a particular resistance), the potential difference across the conductor is proportional to the current.

23. Kirchhoff's junction rule states that the sum of the currents entering a junction equals the sum of the currents exiting the junction.

Kirchhoff's loop rule states that the voltage drops and rises sum to zero going around any closed loop (following a set of sign conventions adopted in a physics text).

24. Hooke's law states that a spring will exert a restoring force, tending toward the equilibrium position, which is proportional to its displacement from equilibrium.

25. Snell's law states that a ray of light will refract towards the normal if it passes into a medium with a higher index of refraction or away from the normal if it passes into a medium with a lower index of refraction. (The equation for Snell's law predicts the precise angle of refraction.)

26. Competitive exclusion principle: If two species compete for the same (limited) resource, they can't both coexist with constant population values. One species will have an advantage, dominating in the long term. The other may become extinct or adapt to a new niche, for example.

27. Pauli exclusion principle: Two electrons in the same atom can't have the same set of quantum numbers.

28. Octet rule: Elements tend to gain, lose, or share electrons in chemical bonding in such a way as to have eight valence electrons. (Although this general rule is very useful, it has exceptions, such as ionic bonds with transition metals.)

29. Doppler effect: When there is relative motion between the source of a wave (such as a sound wave) and an observer, the frequency of the waves as measured by the observer will be different from the frequency of the waves as produced by the source. If the source and observer are getting farther apart, the measured frequency will be lower, and if they are getting closer together, the measured frequency will be higher.

30. Genetic drift refers to a change in the frequency of alleles (in a relatively small gene pool) that occurs by chance (such as by the bottleneck or founder effects).

31. Plate tectonics is the theory that rigid plates in earth's lithosphere slowly move and interact, producing mountains, volcanoes, earthquakes, etc.

32. Continental drift is the hypothesis that the continents were originally part of a supercontinent (the Pangaea) and have slowly drifted apart.

33. Heisenberg's uncertainty principle: The more precisely the position of a particle is measured, the more uncertainty there is in the particle's momentum, and vice-versa. (It's impossible to know its exact position and momentum simultaneously.)

34. Archimedes' principle: When an object is submerged in a fluid, the magnitude of the buoyant force equals the weight of the displaced fluid.

35. Olbers's paradox: If the stars (or galaxies) are distributed uniformly throughout

space, light should be reaching earth from every direction such that the sky should appear uniformly bright. However, the sky isn't uniformly bright at night. (Possible explanations include redshift and the expansion and limited age of the universe.)

36. Conservation of momentum: When the net external force acting on a system is zero, the total momentum of the system remains constant. It is particularly useful to apply this concept to problems that involve collisions or scattering.

37. Conservation of angular momentum: When the net external torque acting on a system is zero, the total angular momentum of the system remains constant.

38. Parallel-axis theorem: If the moment of inertia about an axis passing through the center of a rigid body is known, the moment of inertia about another axis that is parallel to the axis through the center can be found by adding the mass of the rigid body times the square of the distance between these axes.

39. The theory of acquired characteristics is the notion that organisms could acquire traits during their lifetime and pass them on to offspring. (Textbooks label this idea as Lamarckian, though it may not paint a complete picture of Lamarck's theory of evolution, and present this theory in order to offer contrast with Darwin's theory.)

40. Gravitational redshift: An increase in the wavelength of a photon that occurs as the photon travels from a higher gravitational field to a lower gravitational field. (Gravitational redshift is **different** from the Doppler redshift that causes the spectrum of a star to shift as a result of the star moving away from the earth.)

41. The de Broglie relation explains that a particle like an electron exhibits wave-like properties, such that the wavelength is inversely proportional to its momentum.

42. Principle of superposition (in geology): The layers of strata in an undeformed sequence are ordered by age (youngest at the top, oldest at the bottom).

43. Cosmological principle: The distribution of matter in the universe (on a vast scale) should be homogeneous (uniform) and isotropic (the same in all directions).

44. Gauss's law: The net flux of electric field lines passing through a closed surface (even an imaginary one) is proportional to the net charge enclosed by the surface.

45. Ampère's law: The net circulation of magnetic field lines around a closed curve (even an imaginary one) is proportional to the net current passing through the area bounded by the closed curve (by "circulation," we mean the line integral).

46. Fermat's principle: Light tends to follow the path of least time.

47. Faraday's law: A current is induced in a loop of wire when the net magnetic flux passing through the loop changes in time. It is critical to say that it "changes," and for maximum credit you should say "flux" (not "field"). You may discuss inducing an emf rather than a current.

48. Lenz's law: The direction of the current in Faraday's law is such that it tends to oppose the changing magnetic flux. You may discuss an emf rather than a current.

49. Endosymbiotic theory: eukaryotic cells evolved from a symbiotic relationship among a variety of prokaryotes.

50. Galilean relativity: When an object and observers have relative velocities that are very small compared to the speed of light, the velocity of the object to each observer can be found from simple vector subtraction.

51. Einstein's special theory of relativity describes coordinate transformations between observers and objects when the relative velocities are constant, even when the speeds are comparable to the speed of light.

52. Einstein's general theory of relativity describes coordinate transformations between observers and objects when there is acceleration, including acceleration that is created by the gravitational attraction of massive bodies.

53. Graham's law of effusion: The rate of effusion of a gas is inversely proportional to the square root of its molar mass.

54. Markovnikov's rule: When a protic acid HX adds to an asymmetric alkene (or

alkyne), the H of HX bonds to the carbon atom that had the most H atoms.

55. The Stark effect refers to the splitting of spectral lines in the presence of an electric field, while the Zeeman effect refers to splitting in the presence of a magnetic field.

56. Brewster's law: When unpolarized light is incident upon a surface, the reflected ray is completely polarized if the reflected ray is perpendicular to the refracted ray.

57. Malus's law: When polarized light passes through a polarizer, the intensity of light passing through the polarizer is reduced by a factor equal to the square of the cosine of the angle between the original polarization and the axis of the polarizer.

58. Torricelli's law: If a small hole is made in a container of liquid (that is open at the top), the speed of efflux through the hole is the same as if an object had been in free fall from rest along a height equal to the depth of the hole from the top surface.

59. Bernoulli's principle expresses conservation of energy to an ideal fluid for two points along a streamline: The sum of the pressure, kinetic energy per unit volume, and gravitational potential energy per unit volume is constant along the streamline.

60. Principle of faunal succession: The fossils found in the strata of sedimentary rock succeed one another in a definite, determinable order.

61. Photoelectric effect: When light with sufficient frequency is incident upon a metal, electrons are ejected from the surface.

62. Compton effect: When a photon scatters off of an electron that is initially at rest, the wavelength of the photon increases as a result of the interaction (except in the case of a grazing collision where the scattering angle is exactly zero).

63. Henry's law: The solubility of a gas in a solvent is directly proportional to the partial pressure of the gas over the solution.

64. Hess's law: The enthalpy change for a multi-step reaction equals the sum of the enthalpy changes for the individual steps of the reaction. (Enthalpy is an extensive parameter; it is a state function.)

65. Hubble's law: The redshift in the spectra of a distant galaxy is proportional to its distance from earth. You may describe the speed of recession instead of redshift.

66. Hund's rule: For degenerate orbitals (meaning that they have the same energy), one electron is placed in each orbital before electrons are paired. Unpaired electrons have the same spin.

67. The Chandrasekhar limit: The maximum mass of a star (approximately equal to 1.4 solar masses) for which a white dwarf can exist (otherwise, the star would not be able to support electron degeneracy).

68. The Roche limit: If an object (or blob of gas) is held together only by the gravitational attraction of its parts, the object can't be too close to a planet (star, moon, etc.) or it will break apart. This critical distance is known as the Roche limit. (Even a rigid satellite has a minimum distance in order not to break apart from tidal forces.)

69. Bragg's law: The condition for constructive interference for the diffraction of an x-ray by a crystal consisting of parallel planes of atoms is $2d \sin \theta = m\lambda$ (where m is a positive integer and d is the spacing between adjacent planes).

70. Law of DuLong and Petit: At sufficiently high temperatures (above about 300 K), the molar specific heat (at constant volume) of a solid is approximately equal to three times the universal gas constant.

71. Le Châtelier's principle: If a system in equilibrium is disturbed by a spontaneous inhomogeneity or fluctuation in temperature, pressure, or the concentration of a component, the system will tend to return to its original equilibrium condition (provided that the system isn't undergoing a macroscopic change that would affect the equilibrium conditions, such as a piston suddenly made movable).

72. Huygens' principle: Each point on a wavefront serves as a point source for a new set of spherical waves.

73. Wien's law: The wavelength which maximizes the spectral radiance (or emit-

tance) of blackbody radiation is inversely proportional to the absolute temperature. Note: It would be **incorrect** to call it the "maximum wavelength" even though texts call it λ_m. The maximum wavelength is infinite. What λ_m means is the "wavelength for which the spectral radiance is a maximum."

74. Stefan's law: The intensity (or power per unit area) radiated by a black body is proportional to the fourth power of the absolute temperature. Notes: You may call it the radiance (but not spectral radiance) or emittance instead of intensity. Note that we write "blackbody" together as an adjective but "black body" separate as a noun.

75. Meissner effect: All magnetic fields are expelled from the interior of a super-conductor below the critical temperature.

76. Curie's law: The magnetization of a paramagnetic material is directly proportional to the applied magnetic field and inversely proportional to the absolute temperature (for sufficiently high temperatures and low magnetic fields). If you wrote this as an equation, we'll accept it for this answer (the question didn't specify not to).

77. Raoult's law: The partial pressure of a solvent vapor above a solution is equal to the vapor pressure of the pure solvent times the mole fraction of the solvent in the solution. We'll also accept this in equation form for this answer.

78. Weber-Fechner law: In order for two stimuli to be perceived as different, they must differ by some minimum percentage (as opposed to differing by some minimum *amount*). That is, the minimum difference is proportional to the stimulus.

79. Hardy-Weinberg principle: The frequencies of alleles in a population tend to remain constant (unless factors are present to cause the frequencies to change).

80. Price's theorem provides a mathematical formulation of evolution and natural selection.

81. Hall effect: When a current-carrying conductor is in the presence of a magnetic field, a voltage is produced which is perpendicular to the magnetic field and is also

perpendicular to the current.

82. Law of constancy of interfacial angles: For a given crystal (such as a mineral), the angles between corresponding faces are the same (for the same temperature), except for the case of polymorphism.

83. Principle of least action: If a system with fixed energy begins in one state and finishes in another state, the path taken is the one that minimizes the action (which is the integral of the Lagrangian over time). Instead of "minimize," you might refer to "stationary." (This principle is applied to derive equations of motion.)

6 What's That Number?

1. 23 pairs (of chromosomes are contained in one typical human cell)

Note: There are 46 chromosomes, but 23 **pairs**. The question asked about pairs.

2. 0°C and 1 atm (are the temperature and pressure associated with STP)

Note: *This* question didn't specify whether or not to use SI units.

3. 7 (is the pH value for pure water); an acid has a pH value below 7, while a base has a pH value above 7

4. Approximately 2.2 pounds (is the weight of a 1-kg mass near earth's surface)

5. Approximately 29.5 days (relative to the sun, called a synodic month); we'll also accept approximately 27.3 days (relative to the earth, called a sidereal month), since the question didn't specify which; bonus for stating both

6. 6 (is the atomic number of carbon)

7. 4 (is the number of **valence** electrons for a neutral carbon atom)

Note: The question **didn't** ask for the "total" number of electrons (which is 6).

8. 12 amu, exactly (is the mass of the most abundant isotope of carbon, which has six neutrons in its nucleus); the masses of other elements are based on this value

Note: The question **didn't** ask for the average atomic mass of carbon (12.01 amu), which is a weighted average of different isotopes; it specifically asked about carbon 12

9. About 4 light-years (is the distance to our sun's nearest star); Proxima Centauri of the Alpha Centauri system is approximately 4.22 light-years from earth

10. Approximately 20 (kinds of amino acids are found in the human genetic code)

11. 6 (the moon's surface gravity is about 6 times weaker than earth's)

Note: The question **didn't** ask for the value (1.6 m/s^2) of the moon's surface gravity.

12. 2 (bromine, Br, and mercury, Hg)

13. Roughly, 100; there are 118 confirmed as of 2019 (number of elements)

14. 0°C (is the freezing point of water in Celsius)

15. 100°C (is the boiling point of water in Celsius)

16. 32°F (is the freezing point of water in Fahrenheit)

17. 212°F (is the boiling point of water in Fahrenheit)

18. 3.14 (is the value of π to three significant figures); bonus for additional digits

19. 6.02×10^{23} (is Avogadro's number to three significant figures)

20. 3.00×10^8 m/s (is the speed of light in vacuum to three significant figures)

21. 6.63×10^{-34} J·s (is Planck's constant to three significant figures); for this value, the units could be Joules times seconds or they could be Joules per Hertz

22. 9.8 m/s^2 (is earth's surface gravity to two significant figures); note that a third digit is sensitive to a specific location on earth's surface; 32 ft./s^2 is also acceptable

23. $6.67 \times 10^{-11} \text{ N·m}^2/\text{kg}^2$ (is the value of the gravitational constant to three significant figures); this value is a universal constant, unlike the value from Question 22

24. -1.60×10^{-19} C (is the charge of an electron to three significant figures)

Note: The negative sign is critical. Electrons have negative charge.

25. 9.11×10^{-31} kg (is the mass of an electron to three significant figures); one digit would be satisfactory

26. 1.61 (is the value of phi, φ, to three significant figures); two digits will suffice; this value is known as the golden ratio

194

27. Approximately 1000 kg/m³ (is the density of pure water at standard temperature) Note: 1 is incorrect because the question specified SI units (1 g/cm³ = 1000 kg/m³, which is a "fun" and instructive conversion)

28. 1 (is the number of cells contained in one amoeba; it is unicellular)

29. Approximately 70% (of earth's surface is covered with water); before you try to narrow it down further, you must decide whether you want to include fresh water and glaciers, for example

30. Approximately 60%, on average (of water is contained in an adult), if you account for all of the body parts; you also need to decide whether you wish to find the averages weighted by mass or weighted by volume; note that even the bones are significantly "watery," though not nearly as much as most of the other organs

31. Approximately 21%, on average (of earth's atmosphere contains oxygen); however, it varies significantly for the different layers

32. Approximately 78%, on average (of earth's atmosphere contains nitrogen); however, it varies significantly for the different layers

33. 30 (or more precisely, 32, is the number of teeth a typical human adult has)

34. 200 (or more precisely, 206, is the number of bones in a typical adult human)

35. 12 pairs (is the number of pairs of ribs in a typical adult human) Note: There are 24 ribs, but 12 **pairs**. The question asked about pairs.

36. 10⁻¹⁰ m (is the size of a typical atom); an Angstrom is **not** an SI unit; of course, it varies a bit, depending on the element

37. 10⁻¹⁵ m (is the size of a typical atomic nucleus); although a femtometer is **not** an SI unit, it does have a metric prefix combined with an SI unit (so we'll give credit for 1 fm for this answer); again, it varies a bit, depending on the element

38. 5800 K, on average (is the surface temperature of the sun); in Celsius it is about 5500°C, but the question specified **Kelvin**; it may vary over the surface; sunspots

are significantly cooler

39. 14 billion years (is the age of the universe according to science); since it states "roughly," we'll accept anything from 10 to 20 billion (what's a few billion years?)

40. 4.6 billion years (is the age of the earth's sun according to science); we'll accept anything from 4 to 5 billion (but if you said 10 billion, you may have been thinking of the sun's lifetime; it has about 5 billion years left before it becomes a red giant)

41. 7 (periods appear on a standard periodic table); be careful **not** to count the lanthanides and actinides that appear below the table (which are **not** separate periods, but are actually parts of periods 6 and 7)

42. We'll accept anything from 20°C to 25°C (for the standard room temperature), though individual instructors or researchers may prefer a specific value

43. 101,325 Pascals (is standard atmospheric pressure); we'll accept 100,000 Pa; note that the question specified Pascals (**not** atm or kPa, though we'll accept 101 kPa)

44. 1000 (grams are in one kilogram: 1 kg = 1000 g)

45. 100 cm and 1000 mm (are in one meter: 1 m = 100 cm, 1 m = 1000 mm)

46. 10 (millimeters are in one centimeter: 1 cm = 10 mm)

47. 1000 (cubic centimeters are in one liter: 1 L = 1000 cc)

48. 9 (square feet are in one square yard); although there are 3 feet in 1 yard, with area it's different: $1 \text{ yd.}^2 = (3 \text{ ft.})^2 = 3 \text{ ft.} \times 3 \text{ ft.} = 9 \text{ ft.}^2$ (you can see this visually below)

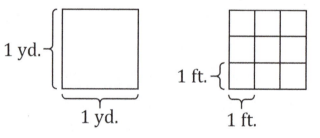

49. 2.54 (centimeters are in one inch: 1 in. = 2.54 cm)

50. 8 (bits are in one byte: 1 byte = 8 bits)

51. 220 (yards are in one furlong: 1 furlong = 220 yds.)

52. 8 (US liquid pints are in one gallon: 1 gal. = 8 pt.)

53. 10,000 times (is how much louder 90 dB is compared to 50 dB); same as 10^4

54. 5 (significant figures are in 0.00032100); the significant figures are 32100; the leading zeroes don't count, but the trailing zeroes do count

55. 2 (small moons orbit Mars: Phobos and Deimos)

56. 10 (is how many electrons the d subshell can hold); the d subshell has 5 orbitals and each orbital can hold two electrons

57. 14 (is how many electrons the f subshell can hold); the f subshell has 7 orbitals and each orbital can hold two electrons

58. the best possible answer is 22 years, on average, but we'll give credit for the popular answer of 11 years (for how long a sunspot cycle lasts); visually monitoring the sun, the pattern lasts an average of 11 years, but if instead you study the cycle knowing that it relates to the sun's magnetic field, you would know that the polarity of the sun's magnetic field reverses every 11 years, such that the 11-year period is actually one-half of the complete sunspot cycle (which is 22 years: 11 + 11 = 22)

59. December 21 and June 21 (are the most common dates for the winter and summer solstices; they can vary by a day or two)

Why do the dates vary? Because the earth takes 365.24 days to complete its orbit, that 0.24 days can cause the date to change. Another complication is the extra day every four years (Leap Year) that helps to correct for that 0.24 days.

60. March 20 and September 23 (are the approximate dates of the vernal and autumnal equinoxes; they can vary by a day or two)

Why are the equinoxes and solstices sometimes on different dates of the month? Because the months don't have exactly 31 days. For example, after June 21, both July and August have a 31st day before September. After December 21, February is a short month (usually 28 days, but occasionally 29).

61. 18th century (is when Benjamin Franklin lived; specifically, 1706–1790)

62. 15th century (is when Leonardo da Vinci was born; specifically, 1452)

63. 1969 (is when Neil Armstrong walked on the moon; specifically, July 20)

64. 16th century (is when Galileo Galilei was born; specifically, 1564)

65. 3rd century BC (is when Archimedes lived; specifically, 287 BC to 212 BC); the BC is critical (as opposed to AD)

66. 17th century (is when Isaac Newton was born; specifically, 1642)

67. 1901 (is when the first Nobel Prizes were awarded)

68. 1636 (is when Harvard was founded, back in colonial times)

69. 340 m/s, approximately (is the speed of sound in air at room temperature); the precise value depends on the pressure and temperature (not specified in the question); we'll accept anything from 330 m/s to 350 m/s (but 760 mph is **not** in SI units)

70. 680 m/s, approximately (is the speed of an airplane traveling Mach 2); if your answer is twice your answer to Question 69, you should receive credit

71. 273 K and 600 Pa, approximately (form the triple point of H_2O); more precisely, the triple point forms at 273.16 K and 611.7 Pa

72. ½ (is the spin of an electron; if you want to be formal, multiply by $\pm\hbar$)

73. 1 (is the spin of a photon)

74. Roughly 60 to 100 beats per minute (is the average adult human heart rate); it's about 1 beat per second

75. 5 (organs of the human body are considered vital: the heart, brain, lungs, liver, and kidneys); perhaps you can make the case for more

76. 40 weeks (is considered full-term); we'll accept 39 to 41

77. About 6 to 7 m for the small intestines, 1.5 m for the large intestines, on average (though it can vary considerably); the adjectives "small" and "large" refer to diameter, not to length (as the small intestine is actually longer)

78. Roughly 0.15 s to 0.25 s (is the average adult reaction time); it also depends on the nature of the stimulus; we'll accept as high as 0.3 s

79. 25 cm (is the near point of the typical, normal adult human eye); if an object is closer than this distance, a typical eye can't focus on it; this varies with age, too

80. 36° to 37°C or 97°F to 99°F (is the normal body temperature of a typical adult)

81. That depends. In 1901, it was 150,000 SEK (Swedish Kronor). It has increased over time. In 2018, it was 9,000,000 SEK. The corresponding values in US dollars are about $20,000 in 1901 and $1.1 million in 2018 (for the value of a Nobel Prize). Currently, a good answer is roughly one million US dollars.

82. Approximately 5700 years (is the half-life of carbon-14); we'll take 5500 to 6000

83. 13.6 eV (is the ionization energy for the ground state of hydrogen); we'll accept 13 to 14 eV, and we're not worried about the sign for this question

84. 105° (is the angle of the H–O–H bond in a polar H_2O molecule); note that this is a little smaller than the 109° angle of a tetrahedron (do a little research if you're interested in why); however, we'll accept anything from 104° to 110°

85. 32 (comes after 2, 8, and 18 in the electron shell model); it's 2 times n^2; these are the number of elements in the periods (rows) of the periodic table (2 in the first, 8 in the second and third, 18 in the fourth and fifth, 32 in the sixth and seventh)

86. 0 and –9.81 m/s^2 (are the horizontal and vertical components of the acceleration of a projectile, assuming it is launched near earth's surface, that air resistance is negligible, neglecting earth's rotation, and assuming a small change in altitude); the horizontal component of the acceleration is zero because a projectile's horizontal component of velocity doesn't change; vertically, there is gravitational acceleration pulling down, which changes the vertical component of velocity; we won't penalize you for this minus sign as long as you "know" that it points downward

87. 1.3 (is the approximate index of refraction for water)

88. G2 (is the stellar classification of the earth's sun); bonus for G2V

89. 6×10^{24} kg (is the approximate mass of the earth); the kg (**not** g) is the SI unit; more precisely, it is 5.9×10^{24} kg, but we'll accept 10^{24} to 10^{25} kg

90. 6×10^{6} m (is the approximate radius of the earth); the m (**not** km) is the SI unit; more precisely, it is 6.4×10^{6} m, but we'll accept 10^{6} to 10^{7} m

91. 4×10^{8} m (is the approximate average earth-moon distance to one significant figure); more precisely, it is 3.8×10^{8} m, but we'll accept 10^{8} to 10^{9} m

92. 100 (is approximately how many times wider the sun is compared to the earth); therefore, about 1,000,000 earths could fit inside of the volume of the sun

How? Because the volume of a sphere is $\frac{4}{3}\pi R^3$. So if R is 100 times larger, R^3 is 100^3 = 100×100×100 = 1,000,000 times larger; thus the volume is 1,000,000 times larger.

93. 5.5 times (is how much more dense the earth is on average compared to water); Saturn is actually less dense on average than water

94. 12 (hydrogen atoms are in present in one molecule of $C_6H_{12}O_6$)

95. 12 (oxygen atoms are present in one "molecule" of $Al_2(SO_4)_3$)

96. $2\,C_6H_{14} + 19\,O_2 \rightarrow 12\,CO_2 + 14\,H_2O$ (is the balanced reaction)

97. $-40°$ (is the same in both Celsius and Fahrenheit); you definitely need to include the minus sign; you can solve for this by setting T_F equal to T_C in $T_F = \frac{9}{5}T_C + 32$; as a check, you can see that $\frac{9}{5}(-40) + 32 = -72 + 32 = -40$

98. 4.186 J of heat (raises the temperature of 1 g of water from 14.5°C to 15.5°C); you should recognize this number either as the specific heat of water, 4186 J/kg/°C = 4.186 J/g/°C, or as the conversion from calories to Joules, 1 cal = 4.186 J, or from the explanation given in textbooks for the mechanical equivalent of heat; we'll accept 4 J

99. About 65 to 70 million years ago (there was a mass extinction event affecting dinosaurs, according to science), associated with an impact in the Yucatán Peninsula

100. 10 (dimensions of spacetime are predicted by superstring theory); we will accept 11 dimensions if you are thinking of M theory, or 9 dimensions for just space (not spacetime); if you said 26, you are thinking of bosonic string theory, whereas the question specified superstring theory

101. 635 to 700 nm (is the approximate range of wavelengths for red light); we'll accept 600 to somewhat over 700 nm; it's equivalent to 6000 to 7000 Angstroms

102. 380 to 450 nm (is the approximate range of wavelengths for violet light); we'll accept a specific value (rather than a range) for these two questions

103. 4 (chambers are found in the stomach of a ruminant such as a giraffe)

104. Roughly 800 to 900 genes on the X chromosome and 50 to 70 genes on the Y chromosome (carry instructions to make proteins); we'll allow a bit of flexibility

105. Roughly 3,000,000,000 or 3 billion (DNA base pairs make up the human genome); we'll accept 1 to 10 billion

106. 4 (are how many wings a typical bee has)

107. About 14 to 15 years (is how long the arctic woolly bear caterpillar can take to reach its full adult moth form); we'll accept anything from 8 to 16 years

108. 3/2 (since $U = \frac{3}{2}nRT$ for a monatomic ideal gas)

109. 5/2 (since $U = \frac{5}{2}nRT$ for a diatomic ideal gas)

110. Approximately 60 earth days (is how long one sidereal "day" lasts on Mercury, meaning one complete rotation on its axis); more precisely, it's 58 to 59 days; don't confuse this with one "year" on Mercury, which is 88 earth "days"

111. Approximately 165 earth years (is how long one sidereal "year" lasts on Neptune); we'll accept 150 to 200 years

112. 3 (is how many generations of quarks and leptons have been discovered); the generations of quarks include up/down, charm/strange, and top/bottom; the three generations of leptons include the electron, muon, tau, and their neutrinos

113. 2/3 (is the charge of an up quark compared to the charge of a proton)

114. –1/3 (is the charge of a down quark compared to the charge of a proton); the negative sign is critical

115. Apollo 11 (is the manned US spaceflight that landed on earth's moon)

116. Roughly 100 to 120 m (is the height of the world's tallest living tree); it's 116 meters, or 380 feet (in the California Redwood forest famous for giant sequoias)

117. Roughly 100 billion (neurons are in a typical adult human brain)

7 What Are Those Units?

1. Kelvin (K) is the SI unit for temperature. Others: Fahrenheit (°F) and Celsius (°C). Note: we don't use the degree (°) symbol for Kelvin because it is "absolute."

2. Pascal (Pa) is the SI unit for pressure, which equates to one N/m^2. Others: atmosphere (atm), bar (bar), pounds per square inch (psi), mm Mercury (mm Hg), torr (torr).

3. Joule (J) is the SI unit for heat. Others: calorie (cal), British thermal unit (Btu), electron Volt (eV), kilowatt hour (kWh), erg (erg), foot-pound (ft.·lb.).

4. Cubic meters (m^3) are the SI units for volume. Others: cubic centimeters (cc), liters (L), cubic feet (ft.^{3}), gallon (gal).

5. Newton (N) is the SI unit for weight. Pound (lb.) is the British unit for weight.

6. Kilogram (kg) is the SI unit for mass. Slug (slug) is the British unit for mass.

7. Atomic mass unit (amu) is defined such that ^{12}C has a mass equal to 12 amu.

8. One Newton (N) equals $kg \cdot \frac{m}{s^2}$. One dyne (dyne) equals $g \cdot \frac{cm}{s^2}$.

9. Radian (rad) is required in the formula for arc length. Other: degree (°).

10. Meter per square second (m/s^2) are the SI units for acceleration.

11. Joule (J) is the SI unit for energy. Others: calorie (cal), British thermal unit (Btu), electron Volt (eV), kilowatt hour (kWh), erg (erg), foot-pound (ft.·lb.).

12. Watt (W) is the SI unit for power. One Watt equals one Joule per second (J/s).

13. Kilogram per cubic meter (kg/m^3) are the SI units for density.

14. One astronomical unit (AU) is equal to the average earth-sun distance.

15. One light-year (ly) is the distance that light travels in one year.

16. One parsec (parsec) is approximately equal to 3.26 light-years.

17. Second (s) is the SI unit for period. Hertz (Hz) is the SI unit for frequency. Note: one Hertz (Hz) is equal to an inverse second (s^{-1}).

18. Energy (or work) may be expressed with the units kWh (but **not** power). Note: Although power is measured in Watts, note that kWh is different because it multiplies by hours (h).

19. Joule (J) is the SI unit for enthalpy. Others: calorie (cal), British thermal unit (Btu), electron Volt (eV), kilowatt hour (kWh), erg (erg), foot-pound (ft.·lb.).

20. Joules per Kelvin (J/K) are the SI units for entropy.

21. The common units are $\frac{\text{Joule}}{\text{kg·K}}$ for specific heat or $\frac{\text{Joule}}{\text{mol·K}}$ for molar specific heat. (For the broad definition of "heat capacity," i.e. not specific, you would get $\frac{J}{K}$, but almost all problems involve specific heat or molar specific heat.)

22. Coulomb (C) is the SI unit for electric charge. It's equivalent to A·s.

23. Ampère (A) is the SI unit for electric current. It's equivalent to C/s.

24. Farad (F) is the SI unit for capacitance.

25. Ohm (Ω) is the SI unit for resistance.

26. Volt (V) is the SI unit for electric potential and for potential difference.

27. Newton per Coulomb (N/C), equivalent to Volt per meter (V/m), are the SI units for electric field.

28. Tesla (T) is the SI unit for magnetic field. Note: Gauss (G) is **not** the SI unit.

29. Joule times second (J·s) are the SI units of Planck's constant. It's equivalent to J/Hz.

30. $\frac{N·m^2}{kg^2}$ are the SI units for the gravitational constant. It's equivalent to $\frac{m^3}{kg·s^2}$.

Note: Question 30 asks for the units of G, whereas Question 31 asks for the units of g.

31. Meter per square second (m/s^2) are the SI units for gravitational acceleration.

32. $\frac{N \cdot m^2}{C^2}$ are the SI units for Coulomb's constant. It's equivalent to $\frac{kg \cdot m^3}{C^2 \cdot s^2}$.

33. Kilogram times meter per second ($kg \cdot m/s$) are the SI units for momentum. It's equivalent to a Newton times a second ($N \cdot s$).

34. Newton times second ($N \cdot s$) are the SI units for impulse. It's equivalent to the SI units for momentum, $kg \cdot m/s$.

35. Newton times meter ($N \cdot m$) are the SI units for torque, but **not** just Newton (N).

36. Kilogram times square meter ($kg \cdot m^2$) are the SI units for moment of inertia.

37. Kilogram times square meter per second ($kg \cdot m^2/s$) are the SI units for angular momentum.

38. None. Trick question: the coefficient of friction is **unitless**.

39. Newton (N) is the SI unit for friction force (or any other kind of force).

40. Decibel (dB) is the SI unit for loudness.

41. Meter (m) is the SI unit for wavelength (or any other kind of distance).

42. None. Trick question: the index of refraction is **unitless**.

43. Candela (cd) is the base SI unit used for luminous intensity.

44. $\frac{N \cdot m^2}{C}$ are the SI units for electric flux. It's equivalent to $\frac{kg \cdot m^3}{C \cdot s^2}$ or $V \cdot m$.

45. The weber (Wb), or equivalently Tesla times square meter ($T \cdot m^2$), is the SI unit for magnetic flux. It's also equivalent to $V \cdot s$.

46. Second (s) is the SI unit for half-life (or any other kind of time).

47. Work or energy may be expressed with units of eV.

48. The times symbol ($\times$) is written after the number for the magnification of a lens. For example, a telescope might have a magnification of $50\times$.

49. $\frac{Joule}{mol \cdot K}$ are the SI units for the universal gas constant. (In some contexts it is convenient to work with other units, but these are the SI units.)

50. Kilograms per square meter (kg/m²) are the SI units for body mass index.

51. Henry (H) is the SI unit for inductance. It's equivalent to $\frac{\text{T·m}^2}{\text{A}}$ or Ω·s.

52. Joule (J) is the SI unit for the work function of a metal (or any other kind of work).

53. $\frac{\text{W}}{\text{m}^2 \cdot \text{K}^4}$ are the SI units for the Stefan-Boltzmann constant (σ).

54. Joule per Kelvin (J/K) are the SI units for Boltzmann's constant (k_B).

55. Becquerel (Bq) is the SI unit for radioactivity.

8 What's That Formula?

1. $W = mg$ relates mass (m) to weight (W).

2. $m = nM$ relates total mass (m) to molar mass (M). Note: n = number of moles.

3. $T_K = T_C + 273.15$ converts from Celsius to Kelvin. (Bonus for the decimals.)

4. $T_F = \frac{9}{5}T_C + 32$ converts from Celsius to Fahrenheit. Note: 9/5 = 1.8.

5. $P = \frac{F}{A}$ relates force to pressure.

6. $P = \rho gh$ relates density to pressure for a fluid. Note: ρ = density. Bonus if you added atmospheric pressure, P_0, according to Pascal's law.

7. $\rho = \frac{m}{V}$ relates mass to density.

8. $M = \frac{\text{moles of solute}}{\text{liter of solution}}$ is the formula for molarity.

9. $m = \frac{\text{moles of solute}}{\text{kg of solvent}}$ is the formula for molality.

10. $\frac{|E-A|}{A}$ 100% is the formula for percent error. Note: E = observed, A = accepted.

11. There are two common conventions for percent difference. One divides by the smaller value, $\frac{|A-B|}{\text{smaller of } A \text{ and } B}$ 100%. The other divides by the average, $\frac{|A-B|}{\frac{A+B}{2}}$ 100%.

12. $PY = \frac{AY}{TY}$ 100% (PY = percent yield, AY = actual yield, TY = theoretical yield).

13. $PE = \frac{(\text{\# of atoms})(\text{element weight})}{\text{formula weight}}$ 100% (PE = percent element).

14. $MP = \frac{CM}{TM} 100\%$ (MP = mass percent, CM = mass of component, TM = total mass of solution)

15. $x = \frac{n_i}{n}$ (x = mole fraction, n_i = moles of component, n = total moles)

16. $v = \frac{d}{t}$ or $d = vt$ is the formula for constant speed.

17. $a_x = \frac{v_x - v_{x0}}{t}$, $\Delta x = v_{x0}t + \frac{1}{2}a_x t^2$, and $v_x^2 = v_{x0}^2 + 2a_x \Delta x$ are for uniform acceleration (the notation may vary, but pay careful attention to the t's, 0's, and squares).

18. $\sum \vec{F} = m\vec{a}$ is Newton's second law of motion.

19. $F = G\frac{m_1 m_2}{r^2}$ is Newton's law of gravity.

20. $F = k\frac{q_1 q_2}{r^2}$ is Coulomb's law.

21. $PV = \text{const.}$ (or $P_1 V_1 = P_2 V_2$) along an isotherm according to Boyle's law.

22. $\frac{V}{T} = \text{const.}$ (or $\frac{V_1}{T_1} = \frac{V_2}{T_2}$) along an isobar according to Charles's law.

23. $PV = nRT$ or $\frac{P_1 V_1}{T_1} = \frac{P_2 V_2}{T_2}$ according to the ideal gas law.

24. $V = \sqrt{V_x^2 + V_y^2}$ is the magnitude of a (2D) vector.

25. $\theta = \tan^{-1}\left(\frac{V_y}{V_x}\right)$ is the direction of a (2D) vector.

26. $f = \frac{1}{T}$ (or $T = \frac{1}{f}$) relates period to frequency.

27. $v = R\omega$ relates angular speed (ω) to speed (v).

28. $a_c = \frac{v^2}{R}$ relates speed to centripetal acceleration.

29. $F_r = -k(x - x_e)$ is Hooke's law. (We'll accept $F_r = -kx$.)

30. $PE_s = \frac{1}{2}k(x - x_e)^2$ is spring potential energy. (We'll accept $PE_s = \frac{1}{2}kx^2$.)

31. $PE_g = mgh$ is gravitational potential energy for a uniform gravitational field. Bonus if you also wrote $PE_g = -G\frac{m_e m}{R}$ for the general case (R is **not** squared).

32. $KE = \frac{1}{2}mv^2$ is kinetic energy. $KE_r = \frac{1}{2}I\omega^2$ is rotational kinetic energy.

33. $W = Fs\cos\theta$ relates force to work if the force and angle are constant. (More

generally, $W = \int_i^f \vec{\mathbf{F}} \cdot d\vec{\mathbf{s}}$.)

34. $P = \frac{W}{t}$ or $P = Fv\cos\theta$ if work is done at a constant rate. (Otherwise, $P = \frac{dW}{dt}$.)

35. $\vec{\mathbf{p}} = m\vec{\mathbf{v}}$ is momentum. $\vec{\mathbf{L}} = I\vec{\boldsymbol{\omega}}$ is angular momentum.

36. $\vec{\mathbf{J}} = \Delta\vec{\mathbf{p}} = m\Delta\vec{\mathbf{v}} = m(\vec{\mathbf{v}} - \vec{\mathbf{v}}_0)$ or $\vec{\mathbf{J}} = \frac{\vec{\mathbf{F}}_{ave}}{t}$ is impulse.

37. $\tau = rF\sin\theta$ or $\tau = F \times$ lever arm relates force to torque.

38. $v = \lambda f$ or $v = \frac{\lambda}{T}$ is wave speed. (If you wrote $v = \frac{\omega}{k}$, that's really cool.)

39. $D = 2R$ relates radius to diameter for a circle. (Missed it? Mandatory facepalm.)

40. $C = 2\pi R$ relates radius to circumference for a circle.

41. $A = \pi R^2$ relates radius to area for a circle.

42. $s = R\theta$ is the arc length for a circular arc.

43. $P = 2L + 2W$ is the perimeter of a rectangle.

44. $A = LW$ is the area of a rectangle.

45. $V = \frac{4}{3}\pi R^3$ is the volume of a sphere.

46. $V = \pi R^2 H$ is the volume of a right circular cylinder.

47. $\Delta V = IR$ is Ohm's law. $P = I\Delta V = I^2 R = \frac{\Delta V^2}{R}$ for power (one is enough).

48. $C = \frac{Q}{\Delta V}$ for capacitance. $U = \frac{Q\Delta V}{2} = \frac{Q^2}{2C} = \frac{C\Delta V^2}{2}$ for energy (one is enough).

49. $\frac{1}{C_s} = \frac{1}{C_1} + \frac{1}{C_2} + \cdots$ for capacitors in series. $C_p = C_1 + C_2 + \cdots$ in parallel.

50. $R_s = R_1 + R_2 + \cdots$ for resistors in series. $\frac{1}{R_p} = \frac{1}{R_1} + \frac{1}{R_2} + \cdots$ in parallel.

Note that the formulas for equivalent capacitance and resistance are "backwards" because $\Delta V = \frac{Q}{C}$ has C "down" whereas $\Delta V = IR$ has R "up." That is, capacitance and resistance play "reciprocal roles" when solving for potential difference (but note that they aren't "actual" reciprocals, since current and charge aren't identical.)

51. $\sigma = \sqrt{\dfrac{(x_1-\bar{x})^2+(x_2-\bar{x})^2+\cdots+(x_N-\bar{x})^2}{N-1}}$ is the standard deviation. Note that (N – 1) is

inside the square root. Not all scientists and engineers use the same form of the standard deviation, so if you know a slightly different formula, it may be okay.

52. $t_{1/2} = -\dfrac{t \ln 2}{\ln\left(\frac{N}{N_0}\right)}$ is the formula for half-life. Alternatively, you could separately use the formulas $t_{1/2} = \dfrac{\ln 2}{k} = \dfrac{0.693}{k}$ and $\ln\left(\dfrac{N}{N_0}\right) = -kt$, where k is the decay rate.

53. $N = N_0 e^{kt}$ is a simple population growth model where k is the reciprocal of the time constant. It can alternatively be expressed as $\ln\left(\dfrac{N}{N_0}\right) = kt$. (Why did the sign change from Question 52 to 53? In Question 52, the sample size decreases over time, whereas in Question 53 the population increases over time.)

54. $AB = \dfrac{L}{4\pi r^2}$ is apparent brightness in terms of luminosity (or power).

55. radians $=$ degrees $\times \dfrac{\pi}{180}$ converts from degrees to radians.

56. $\lambda_m T = \text{const.}$ or $\lambda_m = \dfrac{\text{const.}}{T}$ is Wien's displacement law.

57. $P = \sigma T^4$ is Stefan's law.

58. $E = mc^2$ relates nuclear binding energy to mass difference.

59. $E = hf$ (or $E = nhf$) is Planck's formula for the energy of radiation.

60. $p = \dfrac{h}{\lambda}$ or $\lambda = \dfrac{h}{mv}$ is the de Broglie relation.

61. $\Delta U = Q - W$ is the first law of thermodynamics, where ΔU is the change in internal energy, Q is heat, and W is work. In general, $dU = TdS - PdV + \mu dN$ (for a simple system), which simplifies to $dU = TdS - PdV$ when N is constant.

62. Specific heat: $Q = mC_V(T - T_0)$ if V = const. or $Q = mC_P(T - T_0)$ if P = const. molar specific heat: $Q = nc_V(T - T_0)$ if V = const. or $Q = nc_P(T - T_0)$ if P = const.

63. $Q = mL$ relates heat (Q) to the latent heat (L).

64. $H = U + PV$ is enthalpy. Note: U = internal energy.

65. $\Delta H = H_{prod} - H_{react}$ is the enthalpy change for a reaction.

66. $G = H - TS$ is the Gibbs free energy. Alternatively, $G = U + PV - TS$.

67. $dQ = TdS$ relates entropy to temperature. If T = const., then $\Delta S = \frac{Q}{T}$.

68. $S = k_B \ln \Omega$ relates entropy to the number of microstates.

69. $\Delta L = \alpha L_0 \Delta T$ is the formula for (thermal) linear expansion.

70. $e = \frac{W_{out}}{Q_{in}} = 1 - \frac{|Q_{out}|}{Q_{in}}$ is the efficiency of a heat engine. Specifically for the Carnot cycle, the efficiency becomes $e_C = 1 - \frac{T_c}{T_h}$.

71. $W = P(V - V_0)$ is the work done along an isobar (constant pressure).

72. $\frac{1}{\lambda} = R_H \left(\frac{1}{n_i^2} - \frac{1}{n_f^2} \right)$ is the Rydberg equation for the spectral lines of hydrogen.

73. $N = R_s f_p n_e f_l f_i f_c L$ is Drake's equation.

74. $\vec{F} = q\vec{E}$ relates electric field to force.

75. $E = \frac{\Delta V}{d}$ relates electric field to the voltage between two plates.

76. $F = qvB \sin \theta$ or $F = ILB \sin \theta$ is magnetic force.

77. $\tau = RC$ is the time constant in an RC circuit. It is $\tau = \frac{L}{R}$ for an LR circuit.

78. $T = 2\pi \sqrt{\frac{m}{k}}$ is the period of an oscillating spring.

79. $T \approx 2\pi \sqrt{\frac{L}{g}}$ is the period of a simple pendulum (with a small amplitude).

80. $n = \frac{c}{v}$ is the index of refraction.

81. $n_i \sin \theta_i = n_r \sin \theta_r$ is Snell's law.

82. $f = \frac{v \pm v_o}{v \mp v_s} f_0$ represents the Doppler effect. Note: v = speed of sound.

If the observer is heading toward the source, use + in the numerator.

If the observer is heading away from the source, use – in the numerator.

If the source is heading toward the observer, use – in the denominator.

If the source is heading away from the observer, use + in the denominator.

83. $R = \frac{v_0^2 \sin(2\theta_0)}{g}$ is the range of a projectile if the final position and initial position have the same height.

84. $M_{conc}V_{conc} = M_{dil}V_{dil}$ relates molarities for dilution.

85. $\varphi = \frac{1+\sqrt{5}}{2}$ is the golden ratio.

86. $R = -\frac{1}{a}\frac{\Delta[A]}{\Delta t} = -\frac{1}{b}\frac{\Delta[B]}{\Delta t} = \frac{1}{c}\frac{\Delta[C]}{\Delta t} = \frac{1}{d}\frac{\Delta[D]}{\Delta t}$ the rate of a reaction of the form a A + b B → c C + d D.

87. $R = k[A]^m[B]^n$ is the rate law for a reaction of the form a A + b B → c C + d D.

88. $F_B = m_f g$ is Archimedes' principle; $F_B = \rho_f V g$ is fine, too.

89. $\frac{1}{d_o} + \frac{1}{d_i} = \frac{1}{f}$ relates focal length and image distance for a lens or spherical mirror.

90. $M = \frac{h_i}{h_o}$ or $M = -\frac{d_i}{d_o}$ is the magnification of a lens (or spherical mirror).

91. $\Delta p_x \Delta x \geq \frac{\hbar}{2}$ is Heisenberg's uncertainty principle. Note: $\hbar = \frac{h}{2\pi}$.

92. $I = I_0 \cos^2 \theta$ according to Malus's law.

93. $p = 2aQ$ or $p = dQ$ is the dipole moment, depending on whether you work with the full distance (d) between the charges or the half-distance (a). Note: $d = 2a$. If you wrote $\tau = pE \sin \theta$ or $U = -pE \cos \theta$ instead, this merits credit.

94. $h = \frac{2\gamma \cos \theta}{\rho g R}$ is the height of a meniscus in a cylinder.

95. $\text{pH} = -\log[\text{H}^+]$, $\text{pOH} = -\log[\text{OH}^-]$, and $\text{pH} + \text{pOH} = 14$ (at room temp.).

96. $v_P = \sqrt{\dfrac{\kappa + \frac{4}{3}\mu}{\rho}}$ and $v_S = \sqrt{\dfrac{\mu}{\rho}}$.

97. $M = \mu A D$ is the formula for seismic moment.

98. $X_C = \frac{1}{\omega C}$ for capacitive reactance and $X_L = \omega L$ for inductive reactance ($\omega = 2\pi f$).

99. $\varphi = \tan^{-1}\left(\frac{X_L - X_C}{R}\right)$ is the phase angle for an RLC circuit with AC current.

100. $\lambda_f - \lambda_i = \frac{h}{m_e c}(1 - \cos \theta)$ for the Compton effect.

101. $K = hf - W$ for the photoelectric effect.

102. $p + q = 1$ and $p^2 + 2pq + q^2 = 1$ for the Hardy Weinberg law.

103. $t_d = \dfrac{t_0}{\sqrt{1-\left(\frac{v}{c}\right)^2}}$ for time dilation.

104. $L_c = L_0\sqrt{1 - \left(\frac{v}{c}\right)^2}$ for length contraction.

105. $\chi^2 = \sum \dfrac{(O_i - E_i)^2}{E_i}$ for chi-squared. Note: $(O_i - E_i)^2 = (E_i - O_i)^2$. Why? Since $O_i - E_i = (-1)(E_i - O_i)$ and since $(-1)^2 = 1$.

106. $\phi = \dfrac{V_{void}}{V_{tot}}$ for porosity.

107. $-\dfrac{\hbar^2}{2m}\dfrac{d^2\psi}{dx^2} + V\psi = E\psi$ is Schrödinger's time-independent equation. (Bonus if you also know the time-dependent equation.) The left-hand side is the Hamiltonian operator acting on the wave function. The left-hand side includes both kinetic and potential energy, while the right-hand side includes the total energy. Solving for the wave function allows us to predict various probabilities in quantum mechanics. For credit, at a minimum you should have noted that the wave function is involved and described the significance of the wave function, and how the equation relates to energy (but if you have knowledge of differential equations, for credit you should have been able to write the equation).

108. There are four equations (in integral or differential form):

$\oint_S \vec{E} \cdot d\vec{A} = \dfrac{q_{enc}}{\epsilon_0}$ or $\vec{\nabla} \cdot \vec{E} = \dfrac{\rho}{\epsilon_0}$ is Gauss's law, that the net electric flux through any closed surface is proportional to the charge enclosed by the surface.

$\oint_S \vec{B} \cdot d\vec{A} = 0$ or $\vec{\nabla} \cdot \vec{B} = 0$ reflects that no magnetic monopole has been discovered.

$\oint_C \vec{E} \cdot d\vec{s} = -\dfrac{d\Phi_m}{dt}$ or $\vec{\nabla} \times \vec{E} = -\dfrac{\partial \vec{B}}{\partial t}$ is Faraday's law, that a changing magnetic flux through a loop of wire induces an emf in the loop of wire.

$\oint_C \vec{B} \cdot d\vec{s} = \mu_0 I_{enc} + \epsilon_0\mu_0\dfrac{d\Phi_e}{dt}$ or $\vec{\nabla} \times \vec{B} = \mu_0\vec{J} + \epsilon_0\mu_0\dfrac{\partial \vec{E}}{\partial t}$ is Ampère's law (including Maxwell's addition of the displacement current), that the circulation of magnetic field through any closed loop is proportional to the current enclosed by the loop.

109. $k = Ae^{-Ea/RT}$ is the Arrhenius equation (which may alternatively be expressed using Boltzmann's constant instead of the universal gas constant).

9 What's That Concept?

1. Photosynthesis: Your explanation should mention chlorophyll in plants, sunlight, and the conversion of carbon dioxide and water into carbohydrates and oxygen. The balanced chemical reaction is $6\,CO_2 + 6\,H_2O \rightarrow C_6H_{12}O_6 + 6\,O_2$.

2. Lunar phases: Your explanation should mention sunlight illuminating one-half of the moon's surface, but that depending on the relative position of the earth, sun, and moon, the amount of sunlight seen from earth may vary from 0 (new moon, in which the sun illuminates the side opposite from earth) to 100% (full moon, in which the sun illuminates the side facing earth). Your diagram should show this.

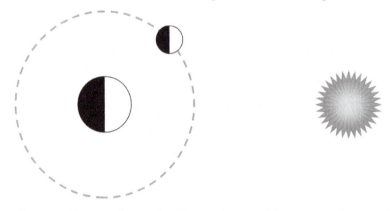

For the diagram shown above, for the position of the moon shown, the lunar phase would be a crescent (less than half of the side of the moon facing earth is illuminated).

3. Earth's seasons are caused by the tilt of earth's axis (**not** by the elliptical nature of earth's orbit). Due to this tilt, in the summer the northern hemisphere receives more direct sunlight (while at the same time the southern hemisphere receives less direct sunlight, which explains why it is winter in the southern hemisphere when it is summer in the northern hemisphere, and vice-versa).

4. Water cycle: Your description should mention the oceans, water vapor in the atmosphere, and ground water. It should also mention evaporation/condensation, precipitation/runoff/seepage, and the role of plants (e.g. transpiration).

5. Earth's pull of the moon: If the moon started from rest, earth's pull would cause it to crash into the earth. Fortunately, the moon isn't starting from rest. It has tangential speed, and it has enough of it to maintain its orbit. In this case, the earth's pull serves as a centripetal force, causing the direction of the moon's velocity to change (but not significantly changing the moon's speed). It would be satisfactory to draw the earth, a tall mountain, projectile orbits, and a satellite orbit, as Galileo did in a famous diagram a few hundred years ago.

6. $E = mc^2$: This equation expresses an equivalence between mass and energy. You should highlight at least one common example, such as its significance in nuclear reactions, the extreme change in rest-mass that occurs in pair annihilation, or the role it plays in the sun providing energy to earth.

7. Metamorphosis: Your description should mention the caterpillar and chrysalis, and should also mention the egg, pupa, larva, and adult.

8. Blood types/transfusions: A, B, AB, and O. The first three carry type A and/or B antigens. Another type of antigen is designated by the Rh factor: Rh^+ carries this, Rh^- doesn't. A successful transfusion does not give a person a new type of antigen. Type A may receive type A or type O, type B may receive type B or type O, type O may only receive type O, and type AB may receive any. However, there is the added restriction of Rh: Rh^- may only receive Rh^- (but Rh^+ may receive Rh^+ or Rh^-). (Note that *plasma* transfusions are different from *blood* transfusions.)

9. Convection: Your description should begin with the hot bottom of the pot heating

the water at the bottom. It should also mention that this heated water at the bottom expands and rises, and that the cooler water at the top is more dense and sinks, and that the volume of the water heats through these convection currents.

10. Greenhouse effect: Your description should mention that certain gases, like CO_2, CH_4, H_2O (vapor), and O_3, in earth's atmosphere influence earth's surface temperature by absorbing heat (analogous to the way that glass traps heat in a greenhouse). You should also state that if the concentrations of these gases increase dramatically, it may increase the average temperature at earth's surface. You might also provide examples of reasons that these concentrations might be changing, such as through the combustion of fuels. (No deductions for stating that this is a complex problem and may not yet be fully understood. But your answer should sound impartial.)

11. Star map: A star map shows the night sky at various times of the year (often by month or by season) for a particular hemisphere (northern or southern). A star map includes compass directions. Hold the star map so that its compass direction and the direction you are actually facing match up (for example, both pointing north). Try to identify constellations. Once you find these, you can search for specific stars. (Phone apps these days greatly simplify this process.)

12. Why the sky is blue: (What we really mean is, when you look above the surface of the earth, why does your eye perceive blue light? The sky itself doesn't have color, but the light entering our eye has color.) The main point in your explanation should mention that shorter wavelengths of light tend to scatter more on average. (Bonus if you know that the intensity of scattered light varies as the inverse of the fourth power of the wavelength.) Your diagram should show at least two different rays of sunlight traveling through earth's atmosphere: One should travel in a straight line, while the other should scatter one or more times. When looking toward the sun, you see light that hasn't scattered, so that light on average is a longer wavelength.

At noon, the sun appears yellow because sunlight has traveled a shorter distance through the atmosphere (those last three words are critical; it's not the overall distance that matters, just the part through the atmosphere) so that less scattering has occurred. At sunrise or sunset, the sun appears red because sunlight has traveled a longer distance through the atmosphere so that more scattering (of all the shorter wavelengths) has occurred (primarily red wavelengths reach your eye in this direction). When you look anywhere in the sky other than the sun, you see blue light because you're looking at an average of scattered light (so these are mostly shorter wavelengths like blue, violet, and green, all averaged together).

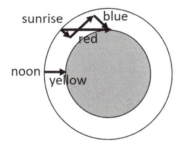

13. Magnet: Your answer should mention the alignment of microscopic magnetic fields (in the form of atomic magnetic dipoles, but if you ascribe this to magnetic fields produced by moving charged particles, we won't ask you to deduct for that), at least partially (as opposed to the random alignment in nonmagnetic materials). If you cut a magnet in half, you get two smaller magnets, and each new magnet has one pair of north and south poles. The idea is that you can't isolate one pole simply by cutting a magnet in pieces. Rather, north and south poles always come in pairs. An isolated pole would be called a magnetic monopole (as of yet undiscovered).

14. Your description should include writing the genotypes of the parents, drawing a table with enough squares for the different gametes possible, labeling the genotypes for the parents, and pairing letters to form genotypes for the gametes. Your description should also mention dominant and recessive alleles, and determining

probabilities. Our example below is for parents who are both Bb, where B = brown eyes and b = blue eyes. Our example has a genotype ratio of 1 BB : 2 Bb : 1 bb and a phenotype ratio of 3 brown : 1 blue (with probabilities of 75% and 25%).

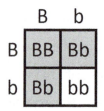

15. Volcano: Your description should mention a build-up of pressure in the earth and the rising of magma, and might also mention tectonic plates, viscosity, and how magma forms. Your description should describe features like the magma chamber and lava flow.

16. Osmosis: One way to illustrate osmotic pressure is to consider a tube with a semi-permeable membrane separating two solutions. You should mention that the solvent will have a net movement towards the solution where the solute is more concentrated. Your description should mention that osmotic pressure is the pressure that must be applied to a pure solvent in order to prevent it from passing into a solution through osmosis. You should also mention one example from biology, such as osmosis in red blood cells or plants absorbing water from the soil.

17. Steel boat: The main idea is that the shape of the boat includes a large volume of air. A steel ball would sink because it is more dense than water. However, air is much less dense than water. Thus, if there is enough air inside the boat that its overall density is less dense than water, the boat will float. You might also discuss buoyancy and Archimedes' principle.

18. Rainbow: Your description should state that the observer stands with his or her back to the sun and that rainbow formation involves the dispersion of sunlight in raindrops. Your diagram should show the refraction and reflection of the red and

violet rays (the two extremes). The red ray emerges from the raindrop at a steeper angle than the violet ray (violet light travels slower than red light in water, so that the violet ray changes direction more). An observer doesn't see red and violet rays leaving the *same* raindrop. Rather, the observer sees red rays coming from a higher angle (because they exit the raindrops at a steeper angle). A secondary, weaker rainbow forms when light enters the bottom of the raindrop and reflects twice inside. The colors of the secondary are reversed compared to the primary.

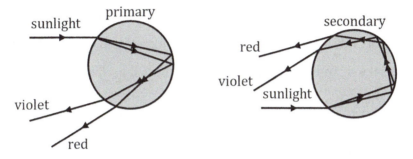

19. Solar eclipses: You should mention that the plane of the moon's orbit around the earth is tilted about 5° compared to the plane of the earth's orbit around the sun. As a result, the moon only crosses the plane of earth's orbit twice every 27.2 days (a draconic month). Compare this to a new moon forming once every 29.5 days (a synodic month). For a solar eclipse to occur, the moon must be close to the earth's orbit during a new moon (otherwise, the earth, moon, and sun won't lie in a straight line and the moon won't be blocking sunlight from reaching earth). Furthermore, even when a solar eclipse does occur, the shadow formed by the moon on earth's surface is only a couple of hundred kilometers wide (note that this shadow moves as the earth rotates and the moon revolves), so only a small portion of the earth will experience a given solar eclipse.

20. Prokaryote and eukaryotic cell: Indicate whether your eukaryotic cell is a plant or animal cell. If it is a plant cell, it should feature a cell wall and chloroplasts but not centrioles, but if it is an animal cell, it should feature centrioles but not chloro-

plasts or a cell wall. A prokaryote should include ribosomes, DNA, a cell wall, and a cell membrane. The eukaryotic cell should also contain other features, such as a nucleus, vacuoles, mitochondria, an endoplasmic reticulum, and Golgi apparatus. See the cell diagrams on the following page (illustrated by Rashi Yadav).

21. Covalent bond in CH_4: The main idea is that hydrogen has 1 valence electron and its outer shell can hold 2, while carbon has 4 valence electrons and its outer shell can hold 8. Therefore, each hydrogen atom in CH_4 shares one **pair** of electrons with the carbon atom (its own electron and one of carbon's valence electrons). By sharing electrons this way, carbon's valence shell is effectively filled with 8 valence electrons (4 pairs make 8) and each hydrogen's valence shell is effectively filled with 2.

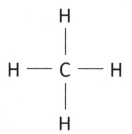

22. Ionic bond in $MgCl_2$: The main idea is that magnesium is a metal with 2 valence electrons, while chlorine is a nonmetal with 7 valence electrons and its outer shell can hold 8. The magnesium atoms each need to lose 2 electrons to have filled outer shells, so they form Mg^{2+}. The chlorine atoms each need to gain 1 electron to have filled outer shells, so they form Cl^- (the 1 is implied). A single Mg^{2+} ion pairs with two Cl^- ions (because magnesium loses 2 electrons and each chlorine gains 1).

23. Life of a main sequence star: You should mention the various stages, including the nebula, protostar, main sequence star, and red giant. The fate of a star depends on its mass. If the core after supernova has less than about 1.4 solar masses it becomes a white dwarf, if it is between about 1.4 and 3 solar masses it becomes a neutron star, and if it exceeds about 3 solar masses it becomes a black hole.

Eukaryotic cell

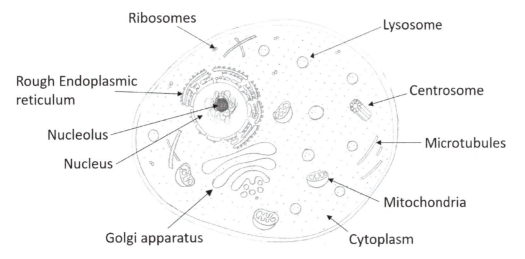

Ribosomes

Lysosome

Rough Endoplasmic
reticulum

Centrosome

Nucleolus

Microtubules

Nucleus

Mitochondria

Golgi apparatus

Cytoplasm

Prokaryotic cell

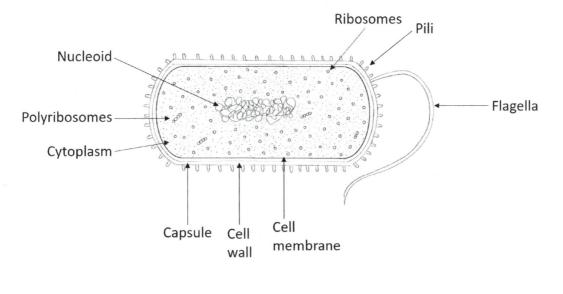

Ribosomes

Pili

Nucleoid

Flagella

Polyribosomes

Cytoplasm

Capsule

Cell
wall

Cell
membrane

24. Rock cycle: Your description should include the five forms (magma, igneous, sediment, sedimentary, metamorphic) and the processes (crystallization, weathering/transport, lithification, metamorphism, and melting – at a minimum).

25. Eukaryotic cell cycle: Your description should include interphase, prophase, metaphase, anaphase, telophase, and cytokinesis, and also describe what each is.

26. Spinning ice skater: The main idea is that she has a smaller moment of inertia when she brings her arms and legs inward, which increases her angular speed such that her angular momentum remains constant. In contrast, she has a larger moment of inertia when she spreads her arms, torso, and one leg outward, which decreases her angular speed in order to conserve her angular momentum.

27. Aerobic exercise and heart disease: You should mention that it makes the heart stronger, increases blood flow, helps keep the blood vessels open, and lowers blood pressure. You might also mention that it prevents clogged arteries and may also help with stress.

28. Tides: The main idea is that the moon exerts a greater force on water that is on the side of the earth that faces the moon and exerts a weaker force on water that is on the side of the earth opposite to the moon (since gravitational force varies with distance), which creates a squeezing effect on earth's oceans (which cover its surface). The parts of the ocean nearest or furthest from the moon experience high tides, and the part of the ocean in between experiences low tides. As the earth rotates on its axis once every 24 hours, different parts of the earth experience low and high tides. In one 24-hour period, any location experiences 2 high and 2 low tides.

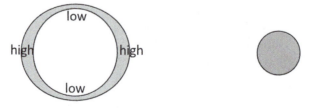

Spring and neap tides each occur twice per month, and have to do with the combined effects of the sun and moon. When the earth, sun, and moon are aligned, the tidal effects are maximum (spring tides). When they form a right angle, the tidal effects are at a minimum (neap tides).

29. Respiratory/circulatory systems: Your description should describe the exchange of gases that occurs between the alveoli and the capillaries, especially the diffusion of oxygen. It should also mention the importance of hemoglobin.

30. Galileo and the heliocentric theory: Galileo observed a range of phases of Venus that aren't possible in the geocentric model. In the heliocentric model, Venus can be on the other side of the sun compared to earth and can experience a full phase, but in the geocentric model Venus and earth are always on the same side of the sun, so Venus can't experience a full phase in the geocentric model. (In the geocentric model, Venus and Mercury are constrained to lie within a cone, as illustrated below, in order to agree with the observation that Mercury and Venus don't stray far from earth's horizon at night. In the heliocentric model, no such cone applies.)

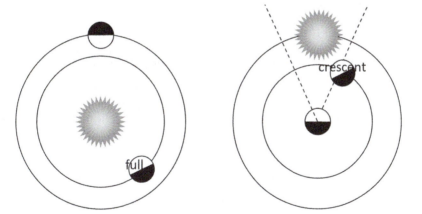

31. Doppler effect: Whereas a stationary source produces concentric wave fronts, a moving source produces off-center wave fronts, as illustrated below. If an observer is in front of the source, the wave fronts are closer together (smaller wavelength, but higher frequency). Behind the source, the wave fronts are farther apart (longer wavelength, but lower frequency).

32. Carbon-14 dating: The main idea is that carbon-14 decays to nitrogen-14 via radioactive beta decay. The reaction is $^{14}_{6}C \rightarrow\ ^{14}_{7}N +\ ^{0}_{-1}e$. The half-life of carbon-14 is 5715 years. When an organism dies, the ratio of carbon-14 to carbon-12 decreases, which allows scientists to estimate the age of organic remains.

33. Mercury thermometer: Your explanation should mention the thermal expansion of mercury, for which the expansion is proportional to the temperature change, and how it is calibrated based on standard measures, such as the freezing and boiling points of water.

34. Carbon: You should mention that carbon has 4 valence electrons and that its outer shell can hold 8, which allows it to form a very wide variety of bonds with many other types of atoms, typically with each carbon atom forming 4 bonds. This helps carbon form strong bonds, and it can even bond with itself. It can form double or triple bonds, and can form chains, rings, and large molecules. (Why is carbon more important for life than silicon, which also has 4 valence electrons? One factor is that carbon bonds tend to be stronger.) An element like carbon that can form very large molecules is essential for making proteins and other substances critical for life.

35. Nitrogen: You should mention the importance of nitrogen for plants (growth, chlorophyll, metabolism), and how the food produced by plants is important for animals.

36. Newton's laws: The second law states that the net force on an object equals its mass times its acceleration. For the special case that the net force equals zero, the second law simplifies to the first law. That is, if the net force is zero, the acceleration is zero, meaning that the velocity is constant.

37. Van der Waals: Gases with high enough density do not obey the ideal gas law as well. The van der Waals equation corrects for this in two ways: It subtracts the volume of the molecules from the volume of the gas, and corrects the pressure by accounting for attractive intermolecular forces.

38. Archimedes' principle: You should state that the buoyant force equals the weight of the displaced fluid. The buoyant force is $F_B = m_f g = \rho_f g V_f$ (where f stands for the fluid). The weight of the object is $m_o g = \rho_o g V_o$ (where o stands for the object). If the object is wholly submerged in the fluid, $V_o = V_f$. The net force equals $F_B - m_f g = \rho_f g V_f - \rho_o g V_o = (\rho_f - \rho_o) g V_o$, which according to Newton's second law equals mass times acceleration. The object accelerates downward (it sinks) if it is more dense than the fluid and accelerates upward (it rises) if it is less dense than the fluid.

39. Tornado: Your description should mention a warm and humid lower atmosphere and cooler upper atmosphere (common in the US in states north of the Gulf of Mexico in spring and early summer), severe thunderstorms, and wind shear.

40. Heat engine: Your description should mention that the natural flow of heat from a thermal reservoir at high temperature to a thermal reservoir at low temperature is adapted in order to perform mechanical work. You should also mention that a heat engine can't be 100% efficient according to the second law of thermodynamics.

10 What's That Abbreviation?

1. STP = standard temperature and air pressure

2. SETI = search for extraterrestrial intelligence

3. SI = le Système International (d'unités), aka the International System (of units)

4. MKS = meter-kilogram-second and CGS = centimeter-gram-second

5. GB = gigabyte(s) and MHz = megahertz

6. Roy G. Biv = red orange yellow green blue indigo violet

7. amu = atomic mass unit(s)

8. AU = astronomical unit(s)

9. HR = heart rate

10. BP = blood pressure

11. bp = boiling point, fp = freezing point, and mp = melting point

12. AC = alternating current and DC = direct current

13. ppm = parts per million and ppb = parts per billion

14. R&D = research and development

15. HAZMAT = hazardous material

16. REM = rapid eye movement

17. pH = pouvoir hydrogène (which literally means "hydrogen power")

18. Ph.D. = Doctor of Philosophy

19. B.S. = Bachelor of Science and M.S. = Master of Science

20. NASA = National Aeronautics and Space Administration

21. CAD = computer-aided design

22. DNA = deoxyribonucleic acid

23. RNA = ribonucleic acid, mRNA = messenger RNA, rRNA = ribosomal RNA, and tRNA = transfer RNA

24. dB = decibel

25. Rx = recipere ("to take," meaning recipe); we'll accept "prescription"

26. JPL = Jet Propulsion Lab

27. NSF = National Science Foundation

28. FBD = free-body diagram

29. SHM = simple harmonic motion

30. eV = electron Volt

31. EKG = elektrokardiogramm, aka electrocardiogram

32. IR = infrared and UV = ultraviolet

33. CT = computerized tomography (scan)

34. GI = gastrointestinal (tract)

35. CPU = central processing unit

36. IP = internet protocol (address)

37. LAN = local area network

38. USB = universal serial bus

39. RAM = random-access memory and ROM = read-only memory

40. ICU = intensive care unit and NICU = neonatal intensive care unit

41. MRI = magnetic resonance imaging

42. TNT = trinitrotoluene

43. A = adenine, G = guanine, C = cytosine, and T = thymine

44. Fe = iron

45. H_2O = water

46. CH_4 = methane

47. NH_3 = ammonia (no credit for "ammonium," which refers to the ion NH_4^+)

48. N_2O_3 = dinitrogen trioxide (correct prefixes are needed)

49. Al_2O_3 = aluminum oxide (no prefixes this time)

50. $CoCl_3$ = cobalt(III) chloride (Roman numeral is needed)

51. $Mg(NO_3)_2$ = magnesium nitrate

52. NH_4F = ammonium fluoride (no credit for "ammonia"; see Question 47)

53. H_2SO_4 = sulfuric acid

54. NaOH = sodium hydroxide

55. RLC = resistor inductor capacitor

56. ANSI = American National Standards Institute

57. ER = endoplasmic reticulum

58. CFC = chlorofluorocarbon

59. SEM = scanning electron microscope and TEM = transmission electron microscope (or microscopy)

60. VLA = Very Large Array

61. LCD = liquid-crystal display

62. LED = light-emitting diode and OLED = organic light-emitting diode; we'll also accept organic EL diode

63. RA = rheumatoid arthritis (**not** "right ascension," since it specified medicine)

64. UTI = urinary tract infection

65. XRT = external radiotherapy; we'll accept "radiotherapy" (**not** "x-ray telescope," since it specified medicine)

66. PTSD = post-traumatic stress disorder

67. CAT = computerized axial tomography and PET = positron emission tomography (scan)

68. URL = uniform resource locator

69. CCD = charge-coupled device

70. NMR = nuclear magnetic resonance

71. HIV = human immunodeficiency virus

72. AIDS = acquired immune deficiency syndrome

73. ESR = electron spin resonance and EPR = electron paramagnetic resonance

74. ATP = adenosine triphosphate (ATP)

75. EM = electromagnetism and TEM = transverse electromagnetic; note that E&M stands for "electricity and magnetism," which is different from "electromagnetism"

76. CR = conditioned response and CS = conditioned stimulus

77. emf = electromotive force

78. PV = pressure-volume (diagram)

79. PVC = polyvinyl chloride

80. cd = candela

81. CNS = central nervous system

82. CNG = compressed natural gas

83. GIS = geographic information system

84. rms = root mean square

85. sonar = sound navigation and ranging

86. radar = radio detecting and ranging

87. COPD = chronic obstructive pulmonary disease

88. DID = dissociative identity disorder

89. NAD^+ = nicotinamide adenine dinucleotide and $NADP^+$ = nicotinamide adenine dinucleotide phosphate

90. SUSY = supersymmetry

91. BIOS = basic input/output system

92. HTML = hypertext markup language

93. HTTP = hypertext transfer protocol and the S in HTTPS stands for secure

94. OSHA = Occupational Safety and Health Administration

95. MSDS = Material Safety Data Sheet

96. USGS = United States Geological Survey

97. QED = quantum electrodynamics

98. QCD = quantum chromodynamics

99. BMI = body mass index

100. EEG = electroencephalogram

101. LASER = light amplification by (the) stimulated emission of radiation

MASER = microwave amplification by (the) stimulated emission of radiation

102. VSEPR = valence-shell electron-pair repulsion (model)

103. ADHD = attention-deficit hyperactivity disorder

104. IEEE = Institute of Electrical and Electronics Engineers

105. SLAC = Stanford Linear Accelerator Center

106. LHC = Large Hadron Collider

107. CERN = originally Conseil Européen pour la Recherche Nucléaire, aka Center for European Nuclear Research or European Organization for Nuclear Research

108. LNG = liquefied natural gas and LPG = liquefied petroleum gas

109. LPN = licensed practical nurse

110. HDL = high-density lipoprotein and LDL = low-density lipoprotein

111. PTH = parathyroid hormone

112. PCR = polymerase chain reaction

113. NTS = not to scale

114. AGN = active galactic nucleus

115. H-R = Hertzsprung-Russell (diagram)

116. CRT = cathode-ray tube

117. FTP = file transfer protocol

118. IRF = inertial reference frame

119. btu = British thermal unit

120. WAIS = Wechsler Adult Intelligence Scale

121. ADH = antidiuretic hormone; we'll accept vasopressin or argipressin

122. BEC = Bose-Einstein condensate

123. GUT = grand unified (field) theory

124. MIC = minimum (or minimal) inhibitory concentration

125. BCS = Bardeen-Cooper-Schrieffer (theory)

126. DVM = Doctor of Veterinary Medicine

127. DVT = deep vein thrombosis

128. PSR = pulsating source of radio (emission); we'll accept pulsar or pulsating source of radiation

129. QSO = quasi-stellar object; we'll accept quasar

130. SQ3R = survey question read retrieve review (which may have variations for reading comprehension, such as read recite review)

131. AMA = American Medical Association

132. ACS = American Chemical Society (**<u>not</u>** American Cancer Society, since it specified chemistry)

133. AAPT = American Association of Physics Teachers

134. ISEF = International Science and Engineering Fair

135. ASCII = American Standard Code for Information Interchange

136. IUPAC = International Union of Pure and Applied Chemistry

137. HDPE = high-density polyethylene

138. CMOS = complementary metal-oxide semiconductor

139. ENSO = El Niño Southern Oscillation

ABOUT THE AUTHOR

Dr. Chris McMullen has over 20 years of experience teaching university physics in California, Oklahoma, Pennsylvania, and Louisiana. Dr. McMullen is also an author of math and science workbooks. Whether in the classroom or as a writer, Dr. McMullen loves sharing knowledge and the art of motivating and engaging students.

The author earned his Ph.D. in phenomenological high-energy physics (particle physics) from Oklahoma State University in 2002. Originally from California, Chris McMullen earned his Master's degree from California State University, Northridge, where his thesis was in the field of electron spin resonance.

As a physics teacher, Dr. McMullen observed that many students lack fluency in fundamental math skills. In an effort to help students of all ages and levels master basic math skills, he published a series of math workbooks on arithmetic, fractions, long division, algebra, geometry, trigonometry, and calculus entitled *Improve Your Math Fluency*. Dr. McMullen has also published a variety of science books, including astronomy, chemistry, and physics workbooks.

Author, Chris McMullen, Ph.D.

PUZZLES

The author of this book, Chris McMullen, enjoys solving puzzles. His favorite puzzle is Kakuro (kind of like a cross between crossword puzzles and Sudoku). He once taught a three-week summer course on puzzles. If you enjoy mathematical pattern puzzles, you might appreciate:

300+ Mathematical Pattern Puzzles

Number Pattern Recognition & Reasoning
- Pattern recognition
- Visual discrimination
- Analytical skills
- Logic and reasoning
- Analogies
- Mathematics

ARITHMETIC

For students who could benefit from additional arithmetic practice:

- Addition, subtraction, multiplication, and division facts
- Multi-digit addition and subtraction
- Addition and subtraction applied to clocks
- Multiplication with 10-20
- Multi-digit multiplication
- Long division with remainders
- Fractions
- Mixed fractions
- Decimals
- Fractions, decimals, and percentages
- Grade 6 math workbook

www.improveyourmathfluency.com

MATH

This series of math workbooks is geared toward practicing essential math skills:

- Algebra
- Geometry
- Trigonometry
- Calculus
- Fractions, decimals, and percentages
- Long division
- Multiplication and division
- Addition and subtraction
- Roman numerals

www.improveyourmathfluency.com

SCIENCE

Dr. McMullen has published a variety of **science** books, including:

- Basic astronomy concepts
- Basic chemistry concepts
- Balancing chemical reactions
- Calculus-based physics textbooks
- Calculus-based physics workbooks
- Calculus-based physics examples
- Trig-based physics workbooks
- Trig-based physics examples
- Creative physics problems
- Modern physics

www.monkeyphysicsblog.wordpress.com

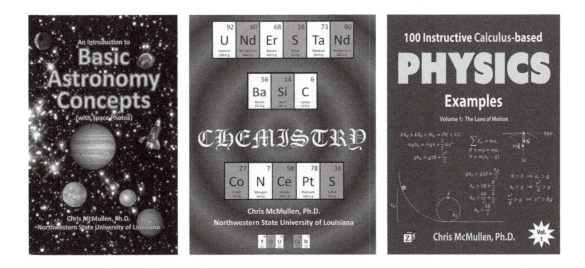

Made in the USA
Las Vegas, NV
01 June 2022

49654749R00129